RUNNING THE RACE OF FAITH

8

week devotional
journal

LIVING A LIFE OF FAITH
AND PURPOSE

Copyright © 2001 Pam Ausenhus
Concordia Publishing House
3558 S. Jefferson Avenue, St. Louis, MO 63118–3968
Manufactured in the United States of America

Library of Congress Cataloging-in-Publication Data

Ausenhus, Pam, 1959–
    Running the race of faith : living a life of faith and purpose : eight-week devotional journal / Pam Ausenhus.
        p. cm.
    ISBN 0-570-05221-0
    1. Students—Prayer books and devotions—English.
2. Devotional calendars. 3. Bible. N.T. Hebrews XII, 12—Criticism, interpretation, etc. [1. Prayer books and devotions.
2. Devotional calendars. 3. Christian life.]   I. Title.
    BV4531.2 .A87 2001
    248.8'3—dc21

                                                    00-011189

1 2 3 4 5 6 7 8 9 10   10 09 08 07 06 05 04 03 02 01

To my husband, Dave,
whose love and encouragement
spur me on in my own race
and whose faithfulness
helps me to see Jesus in so many ways.
You are a priceless gift,
and I count it a privilege
to journey through life by your side.

CONTENTS

INTRODUCTION

Therefore, since we are surrounded by such a great cloud of witnesses ... (Hebrews 12:1)

WEEK 1:

In the Grandstand   14

WEEK 2:

Keeping the End in Mind   36

Let us throw off everything that hinders and the sin that so easily entangles ... (Hebrews 12:1)

And let us run with perseverance the race
marked out for us. (Hebrews 12:1)

> Let us fix our eyes on Jesus, the author and perfecter of our faith, who for the joy set before Him endured the cross, scorning its shame, and sat down at the right hand of the throne of God. (Hebrews 12:2)

INTRODUCTION

Do you ever struggle to find direction or to know that your life is going somewhere that matters? Deep down, most people want to make a difference in the world. We want our lives to count for something of lasting value. What about you? God has made you and put you in this place. What do you see as your purpose, and how do you go about living it out? Where will your journey take you, and what difference will it make? An old saying claims: "Life is like a coin. You can spend it any way you wish, but you can spend it only once." In the pages that follow, we will look at some ways God will empower you to "spend" your life.

Hebrews 12:1–2 has much to say about how we "spend" our lives, and these verses set the tone for this book.

> Therefore, since we are surrounded by such a great cloud of witnesses, let us throw off everything that hinders and the sin that so easily entangles, and let us run with perseverance the race marked out for us. Let us fix our eyes on Jesus, the author and perfecter of our faith, who for the joy set before Him endured the cross, scorning its shame, and sat down at the right hand of the throne of God.

Throughout this book, you will examine the truths of this passage through readings, related Bible verses, personal reflection, and challenges to action. You also will create a statement of purpose and a "spiritual training guide" to help you live out the "heavenly call of God in Christ Jesus" (Philippians 3:14 NRSV) in a life that brings glory to God. In the pages that follow, we will look at parts of Hebrews 12:1–2 and how they apply to our Christian journey as we "run the race of faith."

How to Use This Book

Running the Race of Faith is divided into eight weekly chapters with five devotions in each week. Although this book is meant to be read over a period of eight weeks, feel free to go at any pace that works for you. The devotions may be used for your own personal quiet time or they can be the basis for a group discussion.

Each devotion is followed by some "stretching out" questions designed to help you apply what you read to your life. Space is provided for you to journal your thoughts. Writing your ideas will help to clarify your thoughts and provide a reference to look back on at a later date. At the end of each week, there are some challenge questions labeled "Running the Race," which will encourage you to put what you have learned into action.

Remember that getting the most out of this race cannot be accomplished on your own. Throughout this journey, hold fast to your faith and pray that the Holy Spirit will guide and point you along the paths God would have you take.

> I keep asking that the God of our Lord Jesus Christ, the glorious Father, may give you the Spirit of wisdom and revelation, so that you may know Him better. I pray also that the eyes of your heart may be enlightened in order that you may know the hope to which He has called you, the riches of His glorious inheritance in the saints, and His incomparably great power for us who believe. (Ephesians 1:17-19)

May Jesus bless and guide you as you "run the race of faith"!

Therefore, since we are
surrounded by such a great
cloud of witnesses ...
(Hebrews 12:1)

The first two weeks will focus on this section of
Hebrews 12:1. Commit these words to
memory as a reminder that God does not
leave us to run the race alone. He also does
not leave us without powerful examples of
real people who were as human and imperfect as we are, yet were blessed by God to
live with incredible faith and purpose. We will
look specifically at some of those who have
run the race before us and whose lives
serve as an example and an inspiration as
we run the race of faith.

WEEK 1

IN THE GRANDSTAND

Grandstand Electricity

Imagine that you are running a marathon. You have completed 24 of the 26 miles, and you wonder if you will make it to the finish line. Every bone in your body aches, and you have sore muscles where you didn't even know you had muscles.

As you near the arena where the last mile is to be run, you notice a huge crowd lining the entrance to the stadium. They are cheering, waving, and clapping as each runner nears the complex. Suddenly you realize that you will enter the stadium next, and the crowd is cheering for you! The closer you get, the louder and more excited the crowd grows. You feel a new surge of adrenaline. You pick up your pace, and a smile slowly spreads across your face.

As you pass through the tunnel of cheering voices, you see the inside of the stadium just ahead. It is packed with people. They let out thunderous applause as you enter the arena, and the crowd rises eagerly to its feet. You notice that many people have brought signs bearing words of encouragement ... with your name! Signs wave, streamers fly, and confetti sprinkles the air. The crowd's enthusiasm and energy are contagious. You almost forget how tired you felt a mile or two back.

As you continue to run, the blur of faces comes into focus. You see many people who have influenced your life. They are there to cheer you on. Your mind races wildly as you remember the lessons you learned and the wisdom you gained from them. Tears flood your eyes as you think back to the love, support, and inspiration they brought to your life.

First, you see your sixth-grade teacher, who made each day so much fun! He is that unforgettable man who instilled in you some much needed confidence, a passion for learning, and a commitment to think before you act. His example of faith, lived out in everyday life, remained embedded in your memory, although you didn't understand the full impact until many years later.

Next to him is your high school youth director who never let you take the easy way out. His unrelenting yet gentle insistence that you give your best effort created a commitment to disciplined persistence that has never left you. He also encouraged you to become more involved in worship and Bible study, which God used to draw you closer to Himself.

The next face you see is the wonderful elderly woman who lived next door. Her contagious joy for living and loving always left you inspired and excited to tackle whatever hurdles you were facing at the time. You saw the strength and power of true faith in Christ as the Lord brought her through some difficult times. Her witness helped you see the Lord's guiding hand in your own struggles.

In the front, nearly falling out of their seats, is your family. You now realize in a whole new way the meaning and importance of their constant presence and support. Through them, you have experienced undeserved and unconditional love. Their example of forgiveness and love has given you a sample of what the forgiveness and love of Jesus is like.

As you run a little farther, you see more faces. They look vaguely familiar. You feel like you should recognize them, but you can't quite place their faces. It isn't long, however, before you realize that although you have never physically seen these people, they are the "faithful" whom you have read and studied about—Noah, Sarah, Abraham, Moses, Joshua, Mary and Joseph, John the Baptist, the apostle Paul, and the list goes on. They ran the race before you, and the Holy Spirit guided them through pitfalls and joys. These pillars of faith stumbled and grew weary and knew what it was like to receive new life and strength from God. They have experienced the guidance and grace of God, and they are here to encourage you and to cheer you on.

You are nearing the finish line when your energy begins to fade again and your legs begin to buckle. The crowd notices your struggle and agonizes for you. Their encouragement intensifies in a sincere effort to propel you forward. You appreciate their efforts, but it just isn't enough.

Then you hear another voice. It is strong yet peaceful. *"Look at Me,"* the Voice urges. *"I will give you the strength you need."* You look up, and there at the finish line is Jesus. *"You can do it,"* Jesus encourages as His gaze seems to penetrate into your very soul. *"My strength and power are with you. Keep your eyes focused on Me. Don't turn away. Don't try to do it on your own. You are strong and well trained, but your strength alone is not enough. I have been with you every step of the way, and I will give you what you need to finish the race."*

You see the look of love on His face, and you begin to feel the strength that He promised. With renewed energy, you move steadily toward the finish line. You continue to focus on Him, and your legs feel lighter than they have ever felt. You begin to run faster, and before you know it, you cross the finish line into Jesus' welcoming arms.

He knew you would make it. Long ago, Jesus died to pay for your sins, and He rose to give you this victory.

He sent His Holy Spirit to work faith in your heart and to strengthen you for this race as you read God's Word and dined at His table.

Runners, other athletes, and people in general, are often greatly affected by those who encourage and support them. You probably can think of people who have been there to cheer you on, both when you were running well and during those times that you were worn out, stumbling, or lacking inspiration.

As we run our Christian race and, by the power of the Holy Spirit, seek to follow God's will in our lives, we can draw strength from those who cheer us on, as well as from the people of faith we've never met but whose stories God has included in His Word. Hebrews 12:1 offers a powerful reminder that we are not alone: "Therefore, since we are surrounded by such a great cloud of witnesses. ..."

You may feel like you are surrounded by many people who cheer you on and encourage you, or you may feel like your life is sorely lacking this support. Either way, the Bible reminds us that we all are surrounded by count-less people of faith who have gone before us to mark the course, to provide wisdom, and to cheer us on. Most of all, we gain unlimited strength through the power, forgive-ness, and love of our Lord and Savior, Jesus Christ. He has gone before us and has won the victory through His death and resurrection. He is here beside us now to pro-vide for all our needs.

sTRE T C H I N G oU T

List the names of people who have been there faithfully to cheer you on and to encourage you.

List some specific things they have done to cheer you on.

List the people in your life who have been "people of faith."

List the qualities or actions these people exhibited.

WEEK 1: DAY 2

A Courageous Heart

He was young, and the people of his time assumed that he was not capable of any great act. He was a shepherd boy who normally spent his days wandering the hillsides, tending sheep. On this particular day, the boy's father sent him to check on the safety of his older brothers who were at the battle line. What happened next was both unexpected and unbelievable.

When David arrived at the battlefield, everything seemed to be on hold. In Old Testament times, an army sent their mightiest warrior to challenge the mightiest warrior of the enemy to reduce the lives lost in battle. The champion of this duel could then claim victory for his entire army. This is exactly what was happening when David arrived on the scene.

A giant named Goliath had come forward to challenge anyone from the Israelite army courageous enough to fight him. Goliath was a champion warrior who stood more than nine-feet tall. He was completely covered with heavy armor. He carried a frightful spear and was guarded by a soldier known as a shield bearer. For 40 days, this intimidating giant mocked and challenged the Israelite army to send a warrior to fight him, but Scripture tells us that "When the Israelites saw the man, they all ran from him in great fear" (1 Samuel 17:24).

In comes David. Imagine the reaction when this small, young boy announced to King Saul that he would fight the giant! "David said to Saul, 'Let no one lose heart on account of this Philistine; your servant will go and fight him'" (1 Samuel 17:32). David was willing to step into a situation that left even the bravest and strongest of soldiers shaking in their shoes.

King Saul's first reaction was one of disbelief as he tried to reason with this "foolish" young boy. "Saul replied, 'You are not able to go out against this Philistine and fight him; you are only a boy, and he has been a fighting man from his youth'" (1 Samuel 17:33).

David, however, moved forward with courage, remembering how God had shown him His power and faithfulness in the past. David knew the battle could be won—by the power of God. He stood before Saul and replied: "Your servant has been keeping his father's sheep. When a lion or a bear came and carried off a sheep from the flock, I went after it, struck it and rescued the sheep from its mouth. … The LORD who delivered me from the paw of the lion and the paw of the bear will deliver me from the hand of this Philistine" (1 Samuel 17:34–35, 37). David's courage and persistence won out, and King Saul sent him to battle the great giant.

The events that followed were so unique, so courageous, and so awe-inspiring that this battle has served as an inspiration throughout history. This young, unknown boy, who would one day reign as the king of Israel, was about to become an instrument of God.

> He took his staff in his hand, chose five smooth stones from the stream, put them in the pouch of his shepherd's bag and, with his sling in his hand, approached the Philistine.
>
> Meanwhile, the Philistine, with his shield bearer in front of him, kept coming closer to David. He looked David over and saw that he was only a boy, ruddy and handsome, and he despised him. He said to David, "Am I a dog, that you come at me with sticks?" And the Philistine cursed David by his gods. "Come here," he said, "and I'll give your flesh to the birds of the air and the beasts of the field!"
>
> David said to the Philistine, "You come against me with sword and spear and javelin, but I come against you in the name of the LORD Almighty, the God of the armies of Israel, whom you have defied. This day the LORD will hand you over to me, and I'll strike you down … and the whole world will know that there is a God in Israel. All those gathered here will know that it is not by sword or spear that the LORD

saves; for the battle is the LORD's, and He will give all of you into our hands."

As the Philistine moved closer to attack him, David ran quickly toward the battle line to meet him. Reaching into his bag and taking out a stone, he slung it and struck the Philistine on the forehead. The stone sank into his forehead, and he fell face-down on the ground.

So David triumphed over the Philistine with a sling and a stone; without a sword in his hand he struck down the Philistine and killed him. (I Samuel 17:40-50)

The story of David and Goliath reminds us that the power of God is not limited to how things appear from a human perspective. It challenges us to grab on to the truth that God works through ordinary people whom He has blessed with extraordinary faith. This story shows that it's not a matter of how strong we are on our own; instead, it is a matter of the strength we have been given through faith in the Lord. After all, a meek and humble Jesus was really God. While living on earth among us, He won forgiveness and eternal life for us through His death and resurrection. The example of David's victory demonstrates that it is not who we are, but *whose* we are. David knew the power of God that was available to him. God makes His power available to us too.

David cheers us on from the grandstand as one who knows what it's like to face a "giant-sized" problem with faith and courage. He cheers us on as one who dared to walk where others would not. David walked where others wouldn't because David knew that God had protected him in the past, and would be faithful to do so again. David spurs us on as one who has experienced God's strength in a miraculous way.

Maybe you are facing some "giant-sized" problems of your own. Perhaps you are struggling with fear of rejection or pressure from your peers. Maybe you are experiencing problems in your family or have worries about your grades or feel uncertain about the future. Perhaps you are exhausted and overwhelmed because you are trying to juggle too many things or because you feel as though the expectations placed on you are more than you can possibly live up to.

Remember that if God used a small boy armed only with five smooth stones and a sling shot to kill a giant, He can work just as powerfully in your life. Never forget the ways God has shown His power and faithfulness to you, and never forget that "the battle is the Lord's" [1 Samuel 17:47]!

STRETCHING OUT

List ways God has shown His faithfulness in your life.

What are some "giant-sized" problems in which you need to remember that "the battle is the Lord's"?

How does this story of David inspire you?

A Willing Heart

In a few short minutes, her life changed forever. Her dreams and plans evaporated more quickly than a drop of water in the blazing sun. The unexpected news not only changed her life, but also the entire course of human history.

> In the sixth month, God sent the angel Gabriel to Nazareth, a town in Galilee, to a virgin pledged to be married to a man named Joseph, a descendant of David. The virgin's name was Mary. The angel went to her and said, "Greetings, you who are highly favored! The Lord is with you."
>
> Mary was greatly troubled at his words and wondered what kind of greeting this might be. But the angel said to her, "Do not be afraid, Mary, you have found favor with God. You will be with child and give birth to a son, and you are to give Him the name Jesus. He will be great and will be called the Son of the Most High. The Lord God will give Him the throne of His father David, and He will reign over the house of Jacob forever; His kingdom will never end."
>
> "How will this be," Mary asked the angel, "since I am a virgin?"
>
> The angel answered, "The Holy Spirit will come upon you, and the power of the Most High will overshadow you. So the Holy One to be born will be called the

Son of God. Even Elizabeth your relative is going to have a child in her old age, and she who was said to be barren is in her sixth month. For nothing is impossible with God."

"I am the Lord's servant," Mary answered. "May it be to me as you have said." Then the angel left her. (Luke 1:26-38)

Imagine for a moment what Mary felt. Her day probably started like any ordinary day, but by the time she went to bed that night she had received news that must have made her head swim. She had spoken with an angel and had received a surprising and nearly unbelievable message from God. Mary probably wondered how she would explain her pregnancy to her parents, family, and friends. More important, she probably wondered how Joseph, the man to whom she was engaged, would take the news.

These unexpected circumstances placed Mary in a difficult situation. In Mary's day, an unmarried girl who became pregnant was looked on with disgrace. Unless the father of the child agreed to marry her, she would most likely remain unmarried for life. If her own father rejected her, she could be forced into begging or even prostitution. According to Jewish law, she could even be stoned to death. And Mary, with her story about becoming pregnant by the Holy Spirit, was likely to be suspected of either lying or losing her mind.

Mary's story is a beautiful example of what it means to have a willing heart for the Lord. Although Mary asked questions, her heart was not closed to the plans God had for her no matter how unbelievable or inconvenient. Despite the obstacles before her, the Holy Spirit enabled Mary to undertake what God had in store.

Maybe you, like Mary, have seen your life take an unexpected turn. Perhaps you have received news that was difficult to believe or accept. Maybe you have found yourself asking questions such as: "How can this be possible?" "Is this for real?" or "How could this be happening to me?" Maybe you have felt others looking down on you because of a situation over which you had no control. Perhaps God's plan for your life is different from what you had in mind. Whatever the situation, the forgiveness Jesus earned for you and continually strengthens you with everlasting hope and His divine power.

Mary cheers us on from the grandstand as one who understood what it was like to have life take an unexpected turn. She goes before us as one who understood what it was like to submit to God's will, even when it meant facing trouble. Mary cheers us on as one who has experienced the joy of being used by God to fulfill His holy plans and purposes.

sTRETCHING ouT

What are some unexpected situations you have faced? How did God help you to respond?

What are some questions you have for God right now?

How does Mary's life inspire or encourage you in your approach to dealing with the unexpected?

Read Mary's song of praise to God in Luke 1:46–55, then write your own song to the Lord.

A Compassionate Heart

Do you ever wonder what your purpose is and where Jesus wants to use you? Here is a thought: Maybe *purpose* has less to do with great accomplishments and more to do with how we live and love every day. Perhaps *purpose* has to do with how we spend our time and energy each day with the people who are right in front of our faces. Cheering you on is the story of a man whose compassion reflects the divine compassion Christ shows to each one of us.

> On one occasion an expert in the law stood up to test Jesus. "Teacher," he asked, "what must I do to inherit eternal life?"
>
> "What is written in the Law?" He replied. "How do you read it?"
>
> He answered: "Love the Lord your God with all your heart and with all your soul and with all your strength and with all your mind; and 'Love your neighbor as yourself.'"

"You have answered correctly," Jesus replied. "Do this and you will live."

But he wanted to justify himself, so he asked Jesus, "And who is my neighbor?"

In reply Jesus said: "A man was going down from Jerusalem to Jericho, when he fell into the hands of robbers. They stripped him of his clothes, beat him and went away, leaving him half dead. A priest happened to be going down the same road, and when he saw the man, he passed by on the other side. So too, a Levite, when he came to the place and saw him, passed by on the other side. But a Samaritan, as he traveled, came where the man was; and when he saw him, he took pity on him. He went to him and bandaged his wounds, pouring on oil and wine. Then he put the man on his own donkey, took him to an inn and took care of him. The next day he took out two silver coins and gave them to the innkeeper. 'Look after him,' he said, 'and when I return, I will reimburse you for any extra expense you may have.'

"Which of these three do you think was a neighbor to the man who fell into the hands of robbers?"

The expert in the law replied, "The one who had mercy on him."

Jesus told him, "Go and do likewise." (Luke 10:25-37)

As Jesus told this parable, or story, His listeners would have picked up on one key point. The Samaritan didn't have to stop. He could have followed the examples of the priest and the Levite, who were religious leaders. He could have pretended not to notice the need of the beaten man. It would have been easy to convince himself that someone else would stop to help. The Samaritan could have rationalized that he didn't have the training or medical supplies to care for the man. And because Jews and Samaritans hated each other, he could have reasoned that this Jewish man certainly wouldn't want a Samaritan to help him.

Although the Samaritan could have created dozens of reasons not to stop, he did stop. Because of his compassion and willingness to get involved, a hurting man received care. Because the Samaritan refused to look the other way, grace and kindness became real in the life of a beaten Jewish man and a surprised innkeeper.

The story of the Samaritan is in the Bible to cheer us on and to encourage us. Instead of allowing the attitudes and actions of others to guide us, this parable shows us how the Holy Spirit guides our actions. The story of the Samaritan cheers us because it demonstrates what it means to live with heavenly purpose as we go about everyday acts of compassion and mercy inspired by the unconditional love of Jesus Christ.

You probably can think of times when you were hurting and feeling beat up. Maybe you weren't hurting physically, but you were feeling beat up by criticism or by being left out, rejected, or made fun of. Can you remember what it was like when someone reached out to you in the midst of your hurting and loneliness? Although the world may leave us feeling beat up at times, Jesus reached out to us with love and compassion from the cross. And because we have been baptized into Christ's righteousness, sin no longer can knock us down and rob our lives of God's rich goodness and mercy.

Perhaps you can think of times when you saw someone who was beat up by the unkind or cruel actions of others. You may have struggled with what your response should be. You may have risked reaching out, or you may have passed by the opportunity to help. God asks each of us to reach out with His love and compassion. We have an opportunity to make the message of Christ's love real by how we live. Pray that God will open your eyes to the needs of those around you today. Ask Jesus not only to open your eyes, but also to give you a heart of compassion and a willingness to reach out to those who need help.

sTRETCHING oUT

Describe a time when someone showed compassion when you were hurting.

What are some excuses you use to talk yourself out of reaching out to others?

How does the story of the Good Samaritan inspire you to risk reaching out?

Who could use some compassion right now, and how could you show love and care to this person?

A Servant's Heart

Imagine for a moment that this is your last night on earth. You are spending it with your closest friends. How can you show them how much they mean to you? How can you communicate those things that are of ultimate importance to you? How can you leave them with something that will live beyond you?

Jesus faced just such a time. In His divine wisdom, Jesus left us a loving example to engrave on our hearts and remind us of what it means to be a true servant.

> It was just before the Passover Feast. Jesus knew that the time had come for Him to leave this world and go to the Father. Having loved His own who were in the world, He now showed them the full extent of His love. ... He got up from the meal, took off His outer clothing, and wrapped a towel around His waist. After that, He poured water into a basin and began to wash His disciples' feet, drying them with the towel that was wrapped around Him. ... When He had finished washing their feet, He put on His clothes and returned to His place. "Do you understand what I have done for you?" He asked them. "You call Me 'Teacher' and 'Lord,' and rightly so, for that is what I am. Now that I, your Lord and Teacher, have washed your feet, you also should wash one another's feet. I have set you an example that you should do as I have done for you." (John 13:1, 4-5, 12-15)

Jesus turned the values of the world upside down and inside out. In Jesus' day, the roads were dirt and sand. Because people wore sandals, their feet became extremely dirty, and it was the job of the servants to wash the feet of their master as well as those of his guests. When Jesus took on this role with His disciples, He clearly was breaking tradition, clearly taking on the unexpected and humble role of a servant. Our world tells us to seek power. It also tells us that leadership carries special privileges and the right to be served. Jesus said, "The Son of Man did not come to be served, but to serve, and to give His life as a ransom for many" (Mark 10:45).

Jesus demonstrated a style of leadership that gives up power and chooses to serve with a humble heart. No one cheers us on more than Jesus Himself. His love is so great that He came and lived on earth so we could live with Him forever. Out of His great love, He gave His very life to forgive our sins and the sins of the whole world. He created us, and He longs for us to experience the joy of living out the purpose for which He made us.

Jesus cheers us on as one who knows what it is like to willingly assume the role of a true servant. He urges us forward as one who served friends who had at times disappointed Him and whom He knew would reject Him. In Philippians 2:5–8, we are reminded:

> Your attitude should be the same as that of Christ Jesus: Who, being in very nature God, did not consider equality with God something to be grasped, but made Himself nothing, taking the very nature of a servant, being made in human likeness. And being found in appearance as a man, He humbled Himself and became obedient to death—even death on a cross!

What kind of attitude do you carry into the everyday routine of your life? Maybe you have attained a leadership role at school or church, or perhaps you hope to in the future. That role probably comes with certain privileges or status. How would Jesus have you approach your role? Maybe Jesus has created opportunities for you to serve at your place of work, in your family, in your group of friends, your neighborhood, or your community. How do you respond to these opportunities? When people watch you, do they see a servant's heart?

STRETCHING OUT

How does Jesus' example of servant leadership inspire you?

Who demonstrates servanthood in your life? How do these people demonstrate servanthood?

List some ways the Holy Spirit has inspired you to serve others.

Rate yourself on a scale of 1 to 10

1	2	3	4	5	6	7	8	9	10
pretty selfish								true	servant

How does the Lord enable you to become more of a "true servant"?

RUNNING THE RACE:
CHALLENGE FOR WEEK 1

Memorize the first part of Hebrews 12:1: "Therefore, since
we are surrounded by such a great cloud of witnesses ..."

Write a note of thanks to someone who has influenced your
life and faith.

Write the name of someone you would like to encourage as he or she runs the race of faith.

List ways you can encourage this person. Choose one, and ask God to help you get started! Be sure to continue to encourage this person in the future.

WEEK 2

KEEPING THE END IN MIND

Knowing Your Goal

The score was tied in the championship game with only seconds remaining. An injury to a starting player put Hank into the lineup for the first time all season. He was so excited and nervous that he was sure the other players could see his heart pounding through his jersey.

Hank lined up with the rest of the defense and felt the excitement surging through his veins. The instant the ball was snapped, Hank was on the move. The quarterback dropped back to pass, and the crowd went wild. Immediately, Hank knew that the receiver he was guarding was the intended target. The receiver flashed down the field. Hank's adrenaline kicked in, and he felt as though his feet were flying. He gave it everything he had, but the receiver was just too quick. Disappointment flooded over him as if a dam had broken. Here was his big chance, and he was letting the team down. He couldn't keep pace no matter how hard he tried.

Hank glanced back just as the quarterback released the pass. He thought his eyes were deceiving him, but the ball had been thrown short. Just as the game clock hit zero, Hank jumped and intercepted the ball. Hank knew he only had one chance. He put his head down and ran with blinding speed. He was determined that no one would stop him, and no one did. He was stunned and dazed as he crossed the goal line. Hank had scored ... for the other team.

As we journey through life, it is important to "keep the end in mind." Like Hank, it's easy to get caught up in giving our "all" to the wrong things, only to wake up one day to discover that our efforts have taken us where we would rather not be. If the route is not run to the right goal, every step just gets us closer and closer to the wrong place.

"Keeping the end in mind" means starting with a vision and a destination. It means using your end goal as a filter through which you make choices. People often achieve success that is hollow and empty. They realize the goals they have pursued have come at the expense of things that are more valuable. Imagine how different our lives would be if, by "keeping the end in mind," we would be guided to make daily choices that led to "being" and "doing" what really mattered most.

The apostle Paul is a powerful example of one who lived with a clear goal in mind. He wrote:

> Yet whatever gains I had, these I have come to regard as loss because of Christ. More than that, I regard everything as loss because of the surpassing value of knowing Christ Jesus my Lord. For His sake I have suffered the loss of all things, and I regard them as rubbish, in order that I may gain Christ. ... Not that I have already obtained this or have already reached the goal; but I press on to make it my own, because Christ Jesus has made me His own. Beloved, I do not consider that I have made it my own; but this one thing I do: forgetting what lies behind and straining forward to what lies ahead, I press on toward the goal for the prize of the heavenly call of God in Christ Jesus. (Philippians 3:7-8, 12-14 NRSV)
>
> So I do not run aimlessly, nor do I box as though beating the air. ... (1 Corinthians 9:26 NRSV)

Paul clearly understood his purpose, and he was committed to living out that purpose. By the power of the Holy Spirit, Paul focused on his "end goal" of joining Jesus in heaven. Because of all Jesus had done for him, Paul gave his time and energy to things with eternal value. He lived in a way that helped—not hindered—the spread of the Gospel. After all, Paul knew that Jesus had died on a cross and rose from the dead to provide forgiveness and eternal life for him and all human beings.

Paul "finished well," leaving a legacy of faith for all who have followed. When Paul knew he was nearing the end of his life and that he would soon be killed for his faith, he wrote the following: "I have fought the good fight, I have finished the race, I have kept the faith. Now there is in store for me the crown of righteousness, which the Lord, the righteous Judge, will award to me on that day—and not only to me, but also to all who have longed for His appearing" (2 Timothy 4:7–8). God had used Paul's life to touch others with the saving message of the Gospel. Because of this, Paul knew his life had made an eternal difference. Part of why he "finished well" is because he "kept the end in mind."

We will always face choices, but we can ask God to direct our choices according to His will. What filter do you use in your decisions and choices? Is everything filtered through the cross on which Jesus died for you? Are you asking God to help you live with a sense of purpose and direction? Are you giving your life to things that are temporary or to things that are eternal? When today is over, will you have used it for things that are lasting? When you end this season or this school year, will God be glorified by how you have "spent" this time? And most important, if you died today, would you be able to say with Paul: "I have finished the race, I have kept the faith" (2 Timothy 4:7)?

sTRE T C H I N G oUT

Which of the Bible verses you read today would you like to
keep in mind for your life and why?

List all of the things you did today.

Look over the list you have made and put a T in front of each
thing that has temporary value and an E in front of
things that have lasting or eternal value.
Remember, although an activity itself may not have
eternal value, how you interacted with people during that activity may have lasting value.

List the goals you have, and put a star by the one you con-
sider your top goal. Which of these goals are eternal? Which are temporary?

What are some changes you would ask God to help you
make so more of your life is directed toward things
of eternal value? Pray that the Holy Spirit will help
bring about these changes in your life.

Preparing the Way

Imagine for a moment that you have met some-
one who has radically changed your life. You want to intro-
duce others to this person so their lives might be
changed as well. How will you go about preparing them to
meet this person? How would you describe and talk about
this person? How would you demonstrate the impact that
this person has had on your life?

John the Baptist prepared people to meet the
One who could change lives like no other. John knew that
God created him to announce the coming of the Messiah
and to point people to Him. Keeping this end in mind, God
empowered John to focus his time and energy on making
the world ready to meet Jesus. John was human and
imperfect like the rest of us, but the Holy Spirit had
opened his eyes and given him the words to say. John's
focus was clear, and his goal was in sight.

John's identity was wrapped up in his role as
Christ's messenger. When asked who he was, John
replied: "I am the voice of one calling in the desert, 'Make
straight the way for the Lord' " (John 1:23). In John's day,
when a king was about to travel, a messenger went
ahead to straighten and smooth the roads. In using this
illustration, John called people to prepare not roads but
hearts and lives for the coming of the King of kings. He
challenged people to repent and turn away from their sin.
Hundreds were baptized by John as a symbol of their
repentance, the Holy Spirit having made their hearts
ready for the promised Messiah.

John kept his God-given purpose in the forefront
of his mind and ministry. He never wavered in directing
attention beyond himself and toward Christ. When some

of John's followers were concerned that many went to Jesus for baptism, John's knowledge of his purpose kept him from losing sight of the right goal. John's reply was this: "No one can receive anything except what has been given from heaven. You yourselves are my witnesses that I said, 'I am not the Messiah, but I have been sent ahead of Him'" (John 3:27–28 NRSV). John claimed no greatness and no place for himself; instead, he deflected all honor and attention to Jesus.

While God gives each of us different talents, gifts, abilities, and opportunities, Jesus has given the Great Commission to all people. In Matthew 28:19, Jesus says: "Therefore go and make disciples of all nations." Like John the Baptist, each of us, in our own way, was created to be God's messenger.

Only the Holy Spirit can change people's hearts, but Jesus uses us to prepare His way. You might help to prepare someone's heart as you tell of Christ's faithfulness in your life. You may be able to help someone see that they can receive forgiveness and the promise of eternal life by sharing with them the Gospel message of Jesus' love. Those around you might be drawn to Jesus when you are kind or forgiving, especially when it is undeserved. Jesus might use you to point others to Himself when you help them see the truth of Scripture or when you give credit to the Lord for your success and happiness.

How can you prepare the way for Jesus? How can you live a life that points others to the Savior?

sTReTCHINGouT

List some of the people who have served as mentors in your life.

What are some specific things they did or ways they lived that helped you gain new understanding about your faith in Jesus Christ?

How can you prepare others to meet Jesus or to learn more about Him? How does the Holy Spirit equip you for this task?

How can you live in ways that point others to the Savior?

What role does God's Word play in all of the above questions?

Walking in Faithfulness

Every once in a while, you meet people who just plain stand out in a way that leaves a lasting and profound impression. They know what they stand for, and they aren't afraid to show it. They live for a higher calling, and their example inspires others to do the same. When they die, their lives have made a difference that lives on.

The Bible tells of a man named Joshua, a man known for his faithfulness and conviction. Part of what made him a man to remember was the fact that he knew what he valued most. Keeping this in mind, he refused to be swayed by peer pressure or the temptations of his day. When those around him lost sight of the Lord, Joshua stood out as one who remained steadfast in his commitment to God.

True faithfulness does not happen suddenly. We see in the life of Joshua that true faithfulness is expressed as God empowers the faithful to live in obedience in both the large and the small situations of life. True faithfulness reflects the place of Jesus in one's life—and that place should be first.

Joshua demonstrated a life of honesty and integrity long before God gave him a leadership role. When serving under the great leader Moses, Joshua and 11 others were sent to spy on the land of Canaan and bring back a report so battle plans could be determined. Ten of the spies came back fearful and reported that victory was impossible. Only Joshua and another spy, Caleb, were courageous enough to claim that victory was possible because God was on their side. Although Joshua and Caleb were outnumbered by the other spies, they stood strong against the pressure to conform to their false and fearful message. Although Joshua's report was not honored, he had spoken the truth and had placed his trust in the Lord God.

God recognized Joshua's faithfulness. Following the death of Moses, God chose Joshua to lead the Israelites into the Promised Land. After numerous miraculous victories, the Israelites possessed their homeland. However, despite all God had miraculously provided for these people during their journey out of slavery, many Israelites wandered away from Him and worshiped the false gods of the people they had conquered. It was a time of great turmoil and temptation.

Despite all this chaos, Joshua once again stood firm. He refused to be swayed by the evil of his culture and the choices made by others. He was unswerving in His commitment to the Lord and challenged others to commit themselves to God as well. Joshua's words have resounded in powerful ways throughout history as he stood before the people and boldly proclaimed:

> Now fear the LORD and serve Him with all faithfulness. Throw away the gods your forefathers worshiped beyond the River and in Egypt, and serve the LORD. But if serving the LORD seems undesirable to you, then choose for yourselves this day whom you will serve. ... But as for me and my household, we will serve the LORD. (Joshua 24:14-15)

Joshua could have refused to speak out. He could have remembered that his report was not honored when he was a spy. He could have allowed that experience to cause him to shrink back and keep his thoughts to himself. He could have reasoned that as long as he didn't worship idols, his responsibility stopped there. Instead of giving up, Joshua risked speaking an unpopular message so he could honor the Lord.

Joshua's statement affected the people and brought glory to God. The people responded to his call and turned to the Lord. "And the people said to Joshua, 'We will serve the LORD our God and obey Him'" (Joshua 24:24). Not only did God use Joshua's faith statement to motivate a change of heart and commitment on the part of the Israelites, but the text goes on to say: "Israel served the LORD throughout the lifetime of Joshua and of the elders who outlived him" (Joshua 24:31). The choice to which Joshua called the people and the lifestyle he had faithfully modeled lived on after his death.

Joshua's words challenged the people of his day, and his message challenges us as well: "Choose for your-selves this day whom you will serve. ... But as for me and my household, we will serve the LORD" (Joshua 24:15). We, too, choose who or what takes first place in our lives. There are many today who choose to worship idols. Anything more important than God in our lives becomes an idol. For some it is popularity, achievement, a boyfriend or girlfriend, outward appearance, academics, athletics, money, a hobby, a car, and the list goes on. Many of the worldly messages come in subtle ways that sway our thoughts, and we don't even realize it.

When people look at your life, what do they see? Whom do you worship? If your family and closest friends were asked to name what was number one in your life, what would they say? What message does your life dis-play? Who or what have you chosen to serve first in your life? When people look at you do they see a baptized and forgiven child of God who stands firmly in the faith by the power of the Holy Spirit?

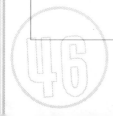

Sometimes it is difficult to determine who or what holds first place in our lives. One test is to recognize how much of our time and money go into certain activities or relationships and compare that to the time and money we devote to the Lord. Estimate how much time you give to Jesus each day or each week.

Estimate the percentage of your money you give to the Lord.

What activities or relationships occupy the most time in your life? (Don't forget to think about how much time you spend on your appearance and on eating because these activities also can become idols.)

On which activities or relationships do you spend the most money?

Which activities or relationships (including your faith relationship with Jesus) get bumped when you are short of time? Which remain priorities?

Looking over your answers to today's questions, who or what holds first place in your life? What changes, if any, would you like to make? How will the Holy Spirit help you make these changes?

WEEK 2: DAY 4

Pursuing the Mission

Even as a 12-year-old boy, He knew He had a unique purpose. He had taken a trip with His parents and a large group of other families. As the group was returning home, His parents suddenly panicked. They assumed their son was somewhere in the large group of travelers, but one day into their journey, they discovered He was nowhere to be found. Like any loving parents, they immediately retraced their steps in hopes of finding their missing son. Three days later, this frantic and exhausted couple found Him in Jerusalem, sitting in the temple and speaking with the teachers. "Why were you searching for Me?" He asked. "Didn't you know I had to be in My Father's house?" (Luke 2:49). Jesus' first recorded words show that, even at a young age, His only concern was to do the will of God His Father.

Jesus lived in faithful obedience. He willingly returned home with His earthly parents, honoring their authority in His life. Jesus also lived in complete submission to His heavenly Father. He clearly proclaimed that His purpose was to do the will of the Father and to live in obedience to the mission that He was sent to fulfill.

> For I have come down from heaven not to do My will but to do the will of Him who sent Me. And this is the will of Him who sent Me, that I shall lose none of all that He has given Me, but raise them up at the last day. For My Father's will is that everyone who looks to the Son and believes in Him shall have eternal life, and I will raise him up at the last day. (John 6:38-40)

Jesus did not live for His own plans and purposes. Although Jesus and the Father are one, Jesus willingly did the Father's will. He listened intently to the voice of the Father and lived according to His guidance and direction. Every word Jesus spoke, every place Jesus went, every miracle He performed intentionally lived out the Father's perfect plan of salvation for all people. Jesus willingly walked into risky and uncomfortable situations. He loved those whom society shunned and touched those considered untouchable. He passionately taught even though He knew His message would threaten those in authority. Jesus faced criticism and false accusations. He gave up material comforts and accepted physical torture. He was willing to do anything to give us the gifts of forgiveness and eternal life.

Everything Jesus taught and lived clearly pointed to His God-given purpose and His commitment to its fulfillment:

> "The Spirit of the Lord is on Me, because He has anointed Me to preach good news to the poor. He

has sent Me to proclaim freedom for the prisoners and recovery of sight for the blind, to release the oppressed, to proclaim the year of the Lord's favor." (Luke 4:18-19)

"I have come that they may have life, and have it to the full." (John 10:10)

"I am the way and the truth and the life. No one comes to the Father except through Me." (John 14:6)

"I have come into the world as a light, so that no one who believes in Me should stay in darkness." (John 12:46)

"For even the Son of Man did not come to be served, but to serve, and to give His life as a ransom for many." (Mark 10:45)

Knowing His purpose and being committed to its fulfillment did not mean that Jesus was immune to human feeling and anxiety. As the time of His death drew near, we know that Jesus was painfully aware of the agony that lay ahead of Him: "'Father, if You are willing, take this cup from Me; yet not My will, but Yours be done.' ... And being in anguish, He prayed more earnestly, and His sweat was like drops of blood falling to the ground" [Luke 22:42, 44]. Fulfilling His purpose was both difficult and costly, but Jesus was determined to obey His Father's will.

For whom do you live? Do you seek to fulfill your own plans and desires, or do you live according to the Father's will? Do you seek to know God's will by regularly spending time in prayer and worship as well as through studying His Word? Are you able to say, like Jesus, "Not my will, but Yours be done"?

sTRETCHING oUT

How did Jesus "keep the end in mind"?

From today's Bible verses, or others with which you are familiar, how would you describe Jesus' purpose?

In what area(s) of your life is it most difficult to say, "Not my will, but Yours be done"?

What sacrifices have you made, or are willing to make, to follow the Lord's will? How does the Holy Spirit empower you to follow Jesus?

WEEK 2: DAY 5

Taking Aim

Imagine what it would be like to run a cross-country race with no idea where the finish line was located or what route you were to take. The "aimless race" might look something like this: You start to run in a direction that you hope is the right way. For a while you follow some runners who seem to know where they are going. As you continue to run, you pass several different paths. Each time you pass a path, you wonder if you are passing the route to the finish line.

Eventually, those you are following begin to head off in separate directions, each claiming they know which way to go. You notice that one has taken a detour into an ice-cream shop and another has taken a trail marked "dead end." You pass by three other trails, and each time, one runner leaves the group and heads off in a new direction. Two of the runners suddenly decide they are so lost that further running is pointless, so they climb into a friend's car that happens to be passing by.

You also begin to wonder what the point of this race is. You're not sure how long you have been running, but you are sure that you're getting tired. There is no finish line in sight. You have no goal. You have no direction. You see no real purpose in continuing.

While such an aimless race would never take place, we are much like the aimless runner if we live without a clear sense of our goal and God-given purpose. Those without a sense of purpose easily become discouraged, confused, or distracted. They often feel as if their lives are going nowhere.

Living with purpose helps us to stay on track and gives us a goal that provides meaning in our lives. It also helps to guide our decisions and to shape the ways we live and love.

Nothing about us is accidental, including the purpose for which we were created. God had a plan for our lives even before we were born. Romans 8:29 says: "For those God foreknew He also predestined to be conformed to the likeness of His Son." We were created to be conformed to the image of Jesus and to be like Him. Through our Baptism, we have been born anew into Christ's holy, perfect image.

Scripture has much to say about the meaning and significance of our lives.

Just as He chose us in Christ before the foundation of the world to be holy and blameless before Him in love. He destined us for adoption as His children through Jesus Christ, according to the good pleasure of His will ... In Christ we have also obtained an inheritance, having been destined according to the purpose of Him ... so that we, who were the first to set our hope on Christ, might live for the praise of His glory. (Ephesians 1:4-5, 11-12 NRSV)

"You did not choose Me, but I chose you and appointed you to go and bear fruit—fruit that will last." (John 15:16)

"Therefore go and make disciples of all nations." (Matthew 28:19)

"Let your light shine before men, that they may see your good deeds and praise your Father in heaven." (Matthew 5:16)

Be imitators of God, therefore, as dearly loved children and live a life of love, just as Christ loved us and gave Himself up for us as a fragrant offering and sacrifice to God. (Ephesians 5:1-2)

To begin with the end in mind, spend some time thinking, reading the Bible, and praying about your purpose and what it means to be conformed to Christ's image. Next, ask yourself these questions:

• What does it mean to live a life that brings glory to God?

• Am I resisting the Holy Spirit as He aligns my life with God's will?

• What is the goal I will keep in mind as I "run the race of faith"?

sTRE T C H I N G oU T

Which of the Bible verses you read were most meaningful to you and why?

What does it mean to be conformed to the likeness of Christ?

What does it mean to live in a way that brings glory to God?

RUNNING THE RACE:
CHALLENGE FOR WEEK 2

Read through the Scripture passages from this week, then search your Bible for others that speak of our purpose in Christ. (Use a Bible with cross-references or a topical Bible.) Spend time in prayer, talking with God. Ask Him to lead you according to His purpose for you.

Write a purpose statement for your life. (If you have trouble, just do the best you can to get started. Refine the statement as God makes His purpose for your life more clear.)

What are you doing to fulfill this purpose? Who and what will help you?

"Keeping the end in mind," pray for the Holy Spirit's help as you set some short-term goals as you start to pursue your purpose.

A goal that I will set for myself for today is:

A goal that I will set for myself for this week is:

Let us throw off everything that
hinders and the sin that so easily
entangles. (Hebrews 12:1)

Jesus will lighten our load and remove the obstacles that can trip us so we are free to run the race of faith. Many of us create unnecessary burdens through the choices we make and the baggage we drag with us. Weeks 3 and 4 challenge us to throw off the excess weight and steer clear of the potholes that would hinder our faith journey.

WEEK 3

CHECK YOUR BAGGAGE HERE

Drop Your Nets

Good runners know that it's foolish to carry extra baggage in a race, to wear too much clothing, or to eat a big meal immediately before running. They know that to finish well, one must be free of unnecessary weight. Sometimes the choices we make weigh us down on our journey of faith. God's invitation is to "let go" and to run the race of faith free from things that would trip us up or weigh us down.

Jesus' disciples were quick to learn the importance of "letting go" as they followed Jesus:

> As Jesus was walking beside the Sea of Galilee, He saw two brothers, Simon called Peter and his brother Andrew. They were casting a net into the lake, for they were fishermen. "Come, follow Me," Jesus said, "and I will make you fishers of men." At once they left their nets and followed Him.
> (Matthew 4:18-20)

Imagine what it would be like to leave your security, your way of life, your comfort zone and follow Jesus into the unknown. The fishermen's nets represented the only way Peter and Andrew knew to make a living. They probably had been fishermen for as long as they could remember. They were trained to be fishermen, and fishing was their comfort zone.

Leaving their nets was necessary to rid themselves of excess weight and bulk. Imagine how ridiculous it would have been for Peter and Andrew to drag their bulky fishing nets on their journeys with Jesus—up mountains, across deserts, through busy cities, and into people's homes. These were not lightweight landing nets! Peter and Andrew probably fished with casting nets. A casting net, which is still used today, is a large, circular-shaped net with a diameter of about nine feet. At the time of Christ, pellets of lead were attached around the outer edges of the net so the net would sink and trap the fish after it was cast.

Dropping their nets meant leaving behind some-thing important in exchange for something even more important—something eternal. Fishing was useful, but Jesus wanted Peter and Andrew to touch lives in ways that would last forever. Jesus wanted them to feed more than people's stomachs. He wanted them to feed people's souls. Peter and Andrew couldn't do all that Jesus want-ed *and* hang on to what was familiar and comfortable.

For these early disciples, leaving their nets involved trusting Jesus to provide all that they needed. Not only did Peter, Andrew, and the other disciples need food and other daily necessities, they also needed training for the ministry to which Jesus had called them. Dropping their nets was a step of faith. By the power of the Holy Spirit, they left behind dependence on their own acquired skill and experience and became wholly dependent on Jesus.

We all sin and hold onto things that weigh us down. Some of these things, like the fishing nets, may have had a purpose. Some might not be bad in and of themselves, yet the place they hold in our lives interferes with our God-given purpose. Finally, there are those things that are simply unhealthy or even destructive; such as the excessive drinking of alcohol, the taking of illegal drugs, and the development of eating disorders.

What "nets" are you dragging around right now? What would Jesus invite you to leave behind so you can follow Him? Maybe it's an unhealthy relationship, the desire to achieve, feelings of guilt or pride, material possessions, bitterness, or a poor self-image. Perhaps you are dragging around disappointment, an addiction of some kind, or the need to handle things on your own. Perhaps you have rejected the free forgiveness from Jesus, leaving yourself heavy with the weight of guilt and sin.

Jesus' call to follow Him comes with an invitation to leave our "nets" behind and to journey into experiences far beyond what we could ever imagine. He already has freed us from sin. Now He wants to free us from those things that would weigh us down or interfere with the journey He has planned for us. Jesus forgives us and leads us to that which is most important. The Holy Spirit moves us to take that step of faith and to place our trust in God alone.

STRETCHING OUT

What things weigh you down? What things does Jesus invite you to leave behind as you follow Him?

What keeps you from letting go?

How do you think your life and faith would be different if you let go of these things?

Leaving Bitterness Behind

Melissa carried a "chip on her shoulder." Her parents had divorced a year earlier, and she had been angry ever since. She resented spending weekends with her dad and away from her friends. She was angry that her allowance had been cut in half because both parents were short of money. As the months passed, Melissa became more and more bitter. Her schoolwork suffered because she just didn't care anymore. She dropped out of choir and decided not to try out for the spring musical. Melissa snapped at her friends over little things, and they gradually started to pull away from her. She vowed that she would never forgive her parents for making such a mess of her life.

While Melissa had reason to feel hurt, her unwillingness to forgive left her with a heavy grudge to carry. The weight of her bitterness seeped into the other parts of her life. The grudge she carried was like a poison that ate away at her heart and spirit.

Jesus knows how important it is for us to forgive, not only for the sake of others but for our sake as well. Although we are forgiven by Christ, when we choose not to forgive others, bitterness and anger build up within us. We drag our grudges around and feel sorry for ourselves. Our lives become infected with resentment, and we lose sight of what we have received—undeserved forgiveness from Jesus.

In Matthew 18:21–35, Jesus provides an important message about forgiveness:

> Then Peter came to Jesus and asked, "Lord, how many times shall I forgive my brother when he sins against me? Up to seven times?"

Jesus answered, "I tell you, not seven times, but seventy-seven times.

"Therefore, the kingdom of heaven is like a king who wanted to settle accounts with his servants. As he began the settlement, a man who owed him ten thousand talents was brought to him. Since he was not able to pay, the master ordered that he and his wife and his children and all that he had be sold to repay the debt.

"The servant fell on his knees before him. 'Be patient with me,' he begged, 'and I will pay back everything.' The servant's master took pity on him, canceled the debt and let him go.

"But when that servant went out, he found one of his fellow servants who owed him a hundred denarii. He grabbed him and began to choke him. 'Pay back what you owe me!' he demanded.

"His fellow servant fell to his knees and begged him, 'Be patient with me, and I will pay you back.'

"But he refused. Instead, he went off and had the man thrown into prison until he could pay the debt. When the other servants saw what had happened, they were greatly distressed and went and told their master everything that had happened.

"Then the master called the servant in. 'You wicked servant,' he said, 'I canceled all that debt of yours because you begged me to. Shouldn't you have had mercy on your fellow servant just as I had on you?' In anger his master turned him over to the jailers to be tortured, until he should pay back all he owed.

> "This is how My heavenly Father will treat each of you unless you forgive your brother from your heart."

The contrast between these debts was huge. The 10,000 talent debt was 500,000 times greater than the 100 denarii owed to the servant! Yet the man who was forgiven the larger amount refused to forgive a smaller debt. By comparison, nothing we forgive can faintly compare with what Christ has forgiven us, yet we often make demands on those in our debt.

To forgive is giving at its deepest level. It starts with Christ and His forgiveness of our sins. Through His forgiveness, we are empowered to give up revenge, repayment, or even justice. In forgiving, we give up a natural mind-set that others are unworthy and unforgivable. Jesus demonstrated what it means to forgive when He paid the price to earn our forgiveness through His suffering and death. Forgiveness is costly, and the cross clearly shows *how* costly. We also remember that true forgiveness is a process that includes making the choice to forgive and allowing the Holy Spirit to make that forgiveness real within us over time. Forgiving is always possible; forgetting is the hard part.

The weight of bitterness easily can become a heavy burden, but God works in our lives through His Holy Spirit so we can forgive others. The essential ingredient is God working within us. In Philippians 2:13, we read: "For it is God who works in you to will and to act according to His good purpose." Whom do you need Jesus to help you to forgive?

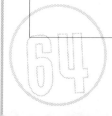

List any grudges you are holding or any people you have not
forgiven.

List any situations in your life that cause you to be angry at
God.

How is bitterness affecting your life and faith?

Write a prayer asking Jesus to help you forgive and to
remove any bitterness you are carrying.

WEEK 3: DAY 3

Giving up Guilt

Imagine you are on a backpacking trip. Along the
path are stones of all shapes and sizes. As you walk, you
think of the many sins you have committed. For each sin,

you pick up a stone and put it in your backpack. You remember the unkind words you spoke to your parents and the little white lie you told to get out of helping a friend. You picture the time you said nothing when you saw another friend making fun of an insecure student and the many times you lost your patience with your younger brother. Your backpack grows heavier and heavier as you continue to add stones. You must stop and rest often because of the great weight you are carrying. Your pack grows bulky and painful. By the end of the day, you are exhausted and wonder how you will ever face tomorrow.

Carrying the weight of guilt is like adding stones to our spiritual backpack. We carry the weight of our sin, even though God provides complete and perfect forgiveness. For many, the weight of guilt becomes not only tiring, but painful. We may carry a heavy burden of sin either because we have not confessed our sin and asked Jesus to forgive us or because we have rejected the forgiveness He offers.

Confession is important not because God needs it, but because we do. Maybe you remember a time that you tried to hide something you had done wrong and felt relief once it was out in the open. Confession cleanses our emotions and removes the weight of guilt as we admit our sins and ask Jesus to forgive us. It is like taking our stone-filled backpack and throwing the stones off the side of a mountain where they fall out of sight and lighten our load. More than that, confession taps into the gift of forgiveness in Christ that puts us in a right relationship with God. We cannot enjoy God's presence in this life or in life after death without the forgiveness that Jesus earned for us through His suffering and death.

Jesus says that if we confess our sins, God will forgive us. In 1 John 1:8–9, we read: "If we claim to be without sin, we deceive ourselves and the truth is not in us. If we confess our sins, He is faithful and just and will forgive us our sins and purify us from all unrighteousness."

When we confess and ask forgiveness, we can trust that we are truly forgiven. There is no need to carry the weight of our sins. The Bible promises that God not only forgives our sins, but also that He forgets our sins. In Isaiah 43:25, God says: "I, even I, am He who blots out your transgressions, for My own sake, and remembers your sins no more." And in Psalm 103:10-12, we read this promise: "He does not treat us as our sins deserve or repay us according to our iniquities. For as high as the heavens are above the earth, so great is His love for those who fear Him; as far as the east is from the west, so far has He removed our transgressions from us."

What are you carrying in your spiritual backpack? Are there unconfessed sins that weigh you down? Do you need to apologize to someone? Are you carrying the painful stones of guilt even though you already have asked God's forgiveness? Do you have a hard time accepting the truth that because of Jesus God has blotted out your confessed sins and erased them from His memory? Jesus will lighten your load and free you from the weight of guilt for your journey of faith.

sTRE T C H I N G oU T

Think about any unconfessed sins you are carrying.

What do you need to confess and ask forgiveness of another person?

List anything you feel guilty about even after asking God to forgive you.

Read through the Bible verses in today's devotion again and copy the parts of those verses that are meaningful to you. Ask Jesus to help you rejoice in His forgiveness.

Confession and forgiveness are followed by a desire to avoid similar sins in the future. How does the Holy Spirit empower you to resist temptation?

WEEK 3: DAY 4
Releasing Worry

We all experience stress and worry. Maybe you are busy and wonder how you will get everything done. Perhaps you worry about the future and all the decisions you face. You might be concerned about your relationships with others and changes that are taking place. Maybe you worry about money, being accepted, or how you look. Worries can fill our lives and burden our hearts, and they can keep us from moving forward in our journey of faith.

We can't choose all our situations because we cannot control our world. We do, however, have choices. Some situations are within our control, such as whether we take our schoolwork seriously or how we treat others. Some situations are outside our control, but we can still choose how we will respond to those circumstances. Someone else may decide whether we make the team or receive a part in the play, but we choose how to act once the decision has been made. We can't control how tall we are, what kind of family we come from, or the choices other people make, but, again, we can choose how we respond.

God has much to say about the pressures we face and the choices we have. The Bible reminds us that Jesus meets us where we are and invites us to experience His perfect faithfulness as we trust Him. In the Bible verses you are about to read, Jesus shares some important truths about what our faith in Him has to offer in the face of worries and concerns.

"Therefore I tell you, do not worry about your life, what you will eat or drink; or about your body, what you will wear. Is not life more important than food, and the body more important than clothes? Look at the birds of the air; they do not sow or reap or store away in barns, and yet your heavenly Father feeds them. Are you not much more valuable than they? Who of you by worrying can add a single hour to his life?

"And why do you worry about clothes? See how the lilies of the field grow. They do not labor or spin. Yet I tell you that not even Solomon in all his splendor was dressed like one of these. If that is how God clothes the grass of the field, which is here today and tomorrow is thrown into the fire, will He not much more clothe you, O you of little faith?

"So do not worry, saying, 'What shall we eat?' or 'What shall we drink?' or 'What shall we wear?' For the pagans run after all these things, and your heavenly Father knows that you need them. But seek first His kingdom and His righteousness, and all these things will be given to you as well. Therefore do not worry about tomorrow, for tomorrow will worry about itself. Each day has enough trouble of its own." (Matthew 6:25-34)

Because we are still sinners, our trust in Jesus is not perfect. At times, it may be hard for you to believe that God is really good or that Jesus is really someone you can trust. Maybe you truly believe that God is trustworthy, but you have a hard time letting go and are still trying to do things on your own. Or it could be that you can trust the Lord in some situations but hold back in others. Jesus said the key is to "seek first His kingdom and His righteousness." You can give your worries to God.

STRETCHING OUT

What illustrations did Jesus use to help us put our worries into perspective?

What things are stressful in your life right now?

What might you change to improve the situation?

How will you ask God to be involved in the process of change?

What do you think it means to "seek first His kingdom and His righteousness"? How will you do that? Who will help you do this?

Overcoming Overcommitments

Imagine you are watching the following scene: It is Saturday morning and Wendy Willing is awakened by the phone. Her friend Susan is calling to see if Wendy will go shopping with her for a prom dress. "Let's see," says Wendy as she checks her calendar. "I have cheerleading practice this morning from 8 o'clock to 10, and then I have piano lessons from 10:30 to 11:30. I promised my little brother that I would go to his soccer game at 1:30, and I'm trying out for the school talent show at 3 o'clock. I have a youth group planning meeting at 4:30 and a birthday party at 5:30. How about if I meet you at noon?"

"Great!" responds Wendy's friend. "I'll see you at the mall."

The doorbell rings, and Wendy's mom tells her Jackie is here to pick her up for cheerleading practice. Wendy rushes to get ready while Jackie helps her throw her extra clothes and piano books into her bag. Wendy quickly returns her phone messages from the night before and writes herself a note to pick up a birthday present when she is at the mall.

Before she leaves her bedroom, the phone rings. Jack is on the phone and wants to know if Wendy would go out with him that night. He'd like to pick her up about 7:30. Wendy has wanted Jack to ask her out for weeks. "That would be fine," Wendy responds. After saying good-bye, she grabs a muffin from the kitchen and rushes off to practice.

Wendy returns from her date at 11 P.M. and gets ready for bed. She lays out materials for the next morning's Sunday school lesson, checks her phone messages, and sets her alarm. Before she can brush her teeth, she falls into a heavy sleep.

Like Wendy, many of us fill our lives with good things—perhaps too many good things. Our calendars overflow and we race from one commitment to the next. *We won't always be this busy or this tired,* we think. *And everything we are doing is important.* But we can become weighed down by overcommitted schedules. When busy schedules push time with Jesus off the calendar, we miss the blessings available to those who are intentional in drawing close to Him. That is when trouble starts. It's difficult enough to be tired from days filled with activity, but when we neglect our spiritual lives, we are in danger of losing more than sleep.

In Luke 10:38–41, Jesus gave us this insight about when being busy is being too busy:

> As Jesus and His disciples were on their way, He came to a village where a woman named Martha opened her home to Him. She had a sister called Mary, who sat at the Lord's feet listening to what He said. But Martha was distracted by all the preparations that had to be made. She came to Him and asked, "Lord, don't you care that my sister has left me to do the work by myself? Tell her to help me!"
>
> "Martha, Martha," the Lord answered, "you are worried and upset about many things, but only one thing is needed. Mary has chosen what is better, and it will not be taken away from her."

Our Lord filled His life with good things and made Himself available to the needs of others, but He took time to be with His heavenly Father. God calls us to give and serve others in His name, but it is important that we remain connected to Him through regular worship, dining at the Lord's Table, and study of His Word so He may enrich our enthusiasm and spiritual strength for our faith journey.

Do you find yourself running from one commitment to the next? Do you often find yourself trying to squeeze in "just one more thing"? Are you feeling the weight and burden of an over-packed schedule? Could Jesus be saying, "Only one thing is needed"?

sTRETCHING oUT

On a scale of 1 to 10, how tired are you?

1   2   3   4   5   6   7   8   9   10

Exhausted   Full of Energy

On a scale of 1–10, what is your current commitment level?

1   2   3   4   5   6   7   8   9   10

Committed to Nothing   Way Overcommitted

What activities need more time? What activities need less?

RUNNING THE RACE:
CHALLENGE FOR WEEK 3

Review your memorization of the first part of Hebrews 12:1: "Therefore, since we are surrounded by such a great cloud of witnesses. ..." Now memorize the second part: "Let us throw off everything that hinders and the sin that so easily entangles ..."

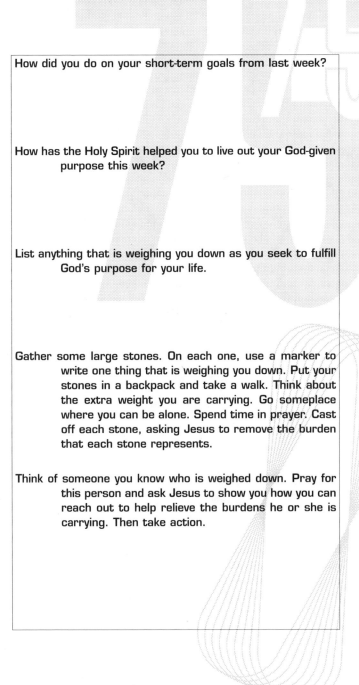

How did you do on your short-term goals from last week?

How has the Holy Spirit helped you to live out your God-given purpose this week?

List anything that is weighing you down as you seek to fulfill God's purpose for your life.

Gather some large stones. On each one, use a marker to write one thing that is weighing you down. Put your stones in a backpack and take a walk. Think about the extra weight you are carrying. Go someplace where you can be alone. Spend time in prayer. Cast off each stone, asking Jesus to remove the burden that each stone represents.

Think of someone you know who is weighed down. Pray for this person and ask Jesus to show you how you can reach out to help relieve the burdens he or she is carrying. Then take action.

WEEK 4

AVOIDING THE TANGLE

The Tangle of Excuses

Ed had been leading the pack for the entire race with Jim following only a short distance behind. As they entered the final leg of the race, Jim picked up his pace and began to close the gap. Ed could sense the pounding of Jim's footsteps just inches behind his own, and he knew that Jim would make his move at any moment. The tired muscles of both runners strained to their limit as Jim slowly took the lead and headed toward the finish line. Jim widened the gap and knew that the race was his when suddenly he stepped into a rut, twisted his ankle, and went down hard.

Anyone who has watched a race in which a runner stumbles and falls knows how quickly an accident can stop even the best athlete. It is equally easy for us to stumble and lose our balance in our journey of faith. We stumble into temptation, or jealousy and greed trip us. Disappointment knocks us off our feet, and peer pressure entangles us. Living a life of faith and purpose requires the Holy Spirit to steer us clear of the potholes and stumbling blocks that can so easily prevent us from accomplishing our goal.

The tangle of our own excuses easily and unexpectedly snags us. We make poor choices, then we start to rationalize our decisions. We make excuses in our day-to-day lives, and we make excuses in our faith walk with Jesus. As we see in the passage below, the rut of excuses can keep us from enjoying God's blessings.

> Jesus replied: "A certain man was preparing a great banquet and invited many guests. At the time of the banquet he sent his servant to tell those who had been invited, 'Come, for everything is now ready.'

"But they all alike began to make excuses. The first said, 'I have just bought a field, and I must go and see it. Please excuse me.'

"Another said, 'I have just bought five yoke of oxen, and I'm on my way to try them out. Please excuse me.'

"Still another said, 'I just got married, so I can't come.'

"The servant came back and reported this to his master. Then the owner of the house became angry and ordered his servant, 'Go out quickly into the streets and alleys of the town and bring in the poor, the crippled, the blind and the lame.'

"'Sir,' the servant said, 'what you ordered has been done, but there is still room.'

"Then the master told his servant, 'Go out to the roads and country lanes and make them come in, so that my house will be full. I tell you, not one of those men who were invited will get a taste of my banquet.'" (Luke 14:16-24)

Those who were offered the invitation in this parable were so tangled up in the things of this world that they turned down the gracious invitation. One by one they made excuses. One by one they refused the feast. And one by one they missed out on the opportunity of a lifetime.

God in heaven has prepared a "great banquet" and invites us to feast on His goodness. Unfortunately, we too make excuses. Like the people in this parable, we often are preoccupied with our earthly desires and tragically pass up God's opportunities and blessings.

Have you ever found yourself promising to start regular devotions as soon as you have more time? Perhaps you tell yourself you can't deal with a hurting friend right now, and you pass up an opportunity to share Jesus' love through your love. Maybe God is inviting you to let go of a bad habit or a sin that causes you to stumble in your faith, and you make excuses to avoid dealing with that part of your life. You may hang out with friends who hinder your Christian faith and rationalize that it really isn't that big of a deal. Or perhaps you tell yourself that you will get serious about your faith when you are older and that now just isn't the time. Whatever it is for you, excuses are stumbling blocks in the race of faith.

In Jesus' parable, as in our lives, Jesus offers an invitation. Jesus invites us to come into His presence and to be filled and satisfied. Will you, like those invitees in the parable, make excuses and be tripped by the things of this world? Or will you feast on His goodness and be united to Him at His Table? We need no excuses with Jesus. He knows our sins and offers us His freely given forgiveness earned on the cross. He comes to us in His body and blood because of His unconditional love for us.

sTRETCHING oUT

Why do you think people say no to God's invitations?

What excuses do you make that hinder your journey of faith?

Imagine you have just received an invitation to the "great banquet" given by Jesus Himself. Write your response below.

The Tangle of Doubt

Maybe you have heard the saying, "The devil made me do it." While Satan can't make us do things, Satan does everything he can to deceive us and knock us out of the race of faith. His ultimate goal is to block the plans and purposes of God. The devil's messages not only are tempting, but deceptive. His lies entangle us, and before we know it, we have tripped and fallen.

In the verses you are about to read, Jesus was tempted by Satan. Notice how He responded to what the devil offered. Note the important "life truths" that Jesus demonstrated for us.

> Then Jesus was led by the Spirit into the desert to be tempted by the devil. After fasting forty days and forty nights, He was hungry. The tempter came to Him and said, "If You are the Son of God, tell these stones to become bread."

Jesus answered, "It is written: 'Man does not live on bread alone, but on every word that comes from the mouth of God.'"

Then the devil took Him to the holy city and had Him stand on the highest point of the temple. "If You are the Son of God," he said, "throw Yourself down. For it is written: 'He will command His angels concerning you, and they will lift you up in their hands, so that you will not strike your foot against a stone.'"

Jesus answered him, "It is also written: 'Do not put the Lord your God to the test.'"

Again, the devil took Him to a very high mountain and showed Him all the kingdoms of the world and their splendor. "All this I will give You," he said, "if You will bow down and worship me."

Jesus said to him, "Away from Me, Satan! For it is written: 'Worship the Lord your God, and serve Him only.'"

Then the devil left Him, and angels came and attended Him. (Matthew 4:1-11)

One of Satan's most powerful tactics is to sow seeds of doubt. Satan tried to trip Jesus by planting an *if* in His mind: "*If* You are the Son of God," or in other words, "*If* You are God's beloved, You don't need to obey Him."

Satan tries to plant an *if* in our minds as well. He tries to make us doubt God's presence, love, and forgiveness. Satan tempts, "*If* God is really good, then why is this painful situation happening?" "*If* God really loves you, then why doesn't He always give you what you ask for?" "You say you're going to trust Jesus, but what *if* He doesn't come through?" Satan encourages us to believe that God does not love us—or that God has abandoned us—when our lives hit rough times.

You may have wondered where God is in times of struggle. In the wilderness of conflict and doubt, remember that God has made you His own in the waters of Baptism and His love is unchanging and unconditional. The voice from heaven does not say, "You are My beloved child *if.* ..." God, in Scripture, says, "I have loved you with an everlasting love" [Jeremiah 31:3].

Satan will do all that he can to stop the spread of the Gospel by distancing us from God, distorting the truth, distracting our attention, and delaying our journey. When you feel tempted to doubt God's goodness and love, be aware that Satan is trying to keep you from following Jesus. Satan is powerful, but God is all-powerful.

Jesus shows us that God's Word is a trustworthy weapon for exposing the lies of Satan. Each time Jesus was tempted, He responded with words from Scripture. Over the next few days, we will look more closely at each of these temptations and Jesus' answer.

God has given us the Holy Scripture. Jesus promises in John 8:32, "Then you will know the truth, and the truth will set you free." The Holy Spirit working through God's Word frees us from the tangle of our doubts and allows us to overcome obstacles that Satan scatters in our path.

sTRETCHING oUT

Identify the lies, doubts, or ifs, you experience.

Write a prayer asking God to help you listen to His voice.

Spend some time in the Bible, listening to God's voice. Try
reading Psalm 139, Jeremiah 29:11–14, and
Isaiah 43:1–3a. Write down the parts of these
verses that are especially meaningful to you.

The Tangle of Instant Gratification

Jack had planned to spend the evening at home
studying for the three exams he faced next week. Some
of the older basketball players soon arrived at the door,
prodding him to go out with them. Before he knew it,
Jack found himself stuffed into a car with several other
players, laughing and joking. He wanted to be accepted by
these popular, fun-loving upperclassmen. Jack didn't know
when he left home, however, that one of the player's parents were gone. Nor did he know that these friends had
decided to party.

What's one party? thought Jack. *After all, you
can't study all the time.* Within an hour, word of the party
had spread, and the house was jammed. Alcohol flowed
freely, and even those who normally appeared quiet and
insecure were relaxed and laughing. Jack knew that if he
were caught drinking, he would be off the basketball
team, but surely one drink wouldn't hurt. Maybe then he
could relax and have a good time with the others.

It is when we are unhappy or concerned about ourselves that we are the most vulnerable to temptation. Jesus had been fasting for 40 days when Satan said, "If You are the Son of God, tell these stones to become bread" (Matthew 4:3). Jesus was hungry, and the devil knew it. Normally, there is nothing wrong with eating. It was wrong in this case, however, because the devil was tempting Jesus to use His power for temporary satisfaction.

The devil is aware of the times we are hungry for love or starving for attention. He knows when we struggle with a strong desire to feel needed, wanted, and accepted. He sees our cravings for success and achievement.

In a variety of ways, we are tempted to settle for immediate satisfaction of our desires at the expense of long-term joy and satisfaction. For some, the temptation is to fulfill physical or sexual desires. For others it is overspending, abusing drugs or alcohol, cheating, lying, developing an eating disorder, and the list goes on. Some of the tragic consequences are immediate; others don't appear for many years.

Satan tells us to live for the moment, to ignore the consequences, and to deny the truth of God's Word. Satan says:

> • "If you can create the right outside image, then it doesn't matter what's going on inside.

> • "If you can get away with something, then it must be okay."

> • "If you don't think too much about the long-term consequences of your choices, then you won't be affected by those choices."

The Holy Spirit will help us respond to Satan's temptation the same way Jesus responded—with God's

Word. Jesus said: "It is written: 'Man does not live on bread alone, but on every word that comes from the mouth of God'" (Matthew 4:4). Filling the "hunger" within us with the things of this world is a hollow and foolish choice. It will only leave us hungry and empty all over again. Only Jesus can fill the deepest hunger in our hearts. He does this through Baptism, Communion, the study of God's Word, and our fellowship with other believers.

What are the *hungers* of your heart? Where are you vulnerable to the lies and schemes of Satan? Are you seeking to fill the "empty" places in your heart with temporary "fixes" or with lasting truth—Jesus Christ? Jesus already has provided for your hunger. He died on the cross and rose again to make you His own, and nothing can take that away from you.

sTRETCHING oUT

What are some personal temptations that have long-term consequences?

What are the *hungers* of your heart?

In what area(s) of your life are you vulnerable to the lies and schemes of Satan?

Do you seek to fill the empty places in your heart with temporary fixes or with Jesus Christ? Give specific examples. How does God's Word fill these empty places?

The Tangle of Distortion

Were you ever misinterpreted? Perhaps the person just misunderstood what you meant, or maybe someone twisted your words around on purpose. We all are aware of how easily our words can take on unintended meaning. Words are powerful, and many messages distort the truth and leave us with false information.

In Jesus' second temptation, Satan tried to manipulate Jesus by giving false meaning to God's Word.

> Then the devil took Him to the holy city and had Him stand on the highest point of the temple. "If You are the Son of God," he said, "throw Yourself down. For it is written: 'He will command His angels concerning you, and they will lift you up in their hands, so that you will not strike your foot against a stone.'" (Matthew 4:5-6)

Satan took words of Scripture from Psalm 91:11–12 and used them out of context, twisting them to distort their meaning. The devil misrepresented them. He tried to manipulate Jesus into thinking that this promise meant it was okay to take unnecessary risks and expect God to come to the rescue.

The devil wants to tempt us in the same way. He tempts us to accept the idea that if God is truly trustworthy, then we should force Him to prove it. The temptation is to believe that if God really loves you, no harm will come to you no matter what you do. It would be like running into the middle of a busy freeway and expecting God to miraculously stop the traffic to keep you safe. This would not be an act of faith; instead, it would be an act of foolishness designed to test God. Sometimes we face challenges to be true to God—not to challenge His faithfulness or to build ourselves up in the eyes of others.

We can be fooled by those who take bits and pieces of Scripture and manipulate them for their own purposes. Our world will try to deceive us by misinterpreting Scripture or taking the promises of God and giving them false meaning. This reminds us of how important it is to study the Word of God carefully.

Ephesians 6 refers to the Word of God as the "sword of the Spirit" (Ephesians 6:17). Jesus used this "sword" to expose Satan's lies and manipulations. "Jesus answered him, 'It is also written: "Do not put the Lord your God to the test"'" (Matthew 4:7).

As we run our race of faith, we can trust the Lord and His Word. To do this, we must know what the Bible says. Do you read and study Scripture so you can distinguish truth from lies? Do you look at the Bible as a whole rather than picking out bits and pieces that fit what you want to hear? Do you believe Satan's lie that God must prove Himself to show His faithfulness? Do you fall for Satan's lie that you must do something to earn forgiveness? Do you find yourself testing God, or do you, by the power of the Holy Spirit, respond to false manipulations with the truth and confidence of God's Word?

STRETCHING OUT

How is Scripture sometimes twisted or misrepresented to rationalize certain decisions?

What are some ways that our world tries to give a false picture of who God is and what He promises?

How do people test God and challenge Him to prove His love and faithfulness?

What are some Bible verses you can turn to in response to these lies?

The Tangle of Materialism

Messages designed to make us believe that we need "more" bombard us every day. Our culture places great value on money, possessions, and earthly wealth. Advertisers work hard to convince us that we are missing something—their product. They paint pictures of the "good life" that can be ours if we have the right things and look the right way. Advertisers make all kinds of promises, but in reality they are determined to leave us feeling dissatisfied and wanting more.

Jesus made it clear that material things will never satisfy our deepest longings, yet we get caught up in the desire to have more, do more, and buy more. In the following passage, Jesus shares the key to finding real and lasting riches:

> A certain ruler asked [Jesus], "Good Teacher, what must I do to inherit eternal life?" ...
>
> Jesus answered, "... You know the commandments: 'Do not commit adultery, do not murder, do not steal, do not give false testimony, honor your father and mother.'"
>
> "All these I have kept since I was a boy," he said.
>
> When Jesus heard this, He said to him, "You still lack one thing. Sell everything you have and give to the poor, and you will have treasure in heaven. Then come, follow Me."
>
> When he heard this, he became very sad, because he was a man of great wealth. Jesus looked at him and said, "How hard it is for the rich to enter the kingdom of God. Indeed, it is easier for a camel to go

> through the eye of a needle than for a rich man to enter the kingdom of God." (Luke 18:18-25)

Wealth was not the problem. The problem was that the man's earthly riches were more important to him than God. Jesus asked the man to put God and His kingdom first. He asked him to share his earthly wealth with those who were in need. Jesus does not ask people to give up their material wealth, but He does ask us to let go of anything that gets in the way of our faith in Him.

Jesus' third temptation was to compromise and give first place to someone or something other than God. We read:

> Again, the devil took Him to a very high mountain and showed Him all the kingdoms of the world and their splendor. "All this I will give You," he said, "if You will bow down and worship me."

> Jesus said to him, "Away from Me, Satan! For it is written: 'Worship the Lord your God, and serve Him only.'" (Matthew 4:8-10)

The devil knows that the things of this world look good and can quickly create false needs and desires within us. While it is not true for everyone, possessions and money tend to draw people away from God. In Matthew 6:24, we read: "No one can serve two masters. Either he will hate the one and love the other, or he will be devoted to the one and despise the other. You cannot serve both God and Money."

When money and possessions become overly important, they become our gods. The desire to obtain a certain possession may cause us to become selfish in our giving to others. That desire may cause us to put much time and energy into obtaining that item at the expense of our integrity or our time with God. For many people, the more they have, the more they want, and they become driven to accumulate more and more. Others find security in money or possessions rather than trusting God to provide for their needs.

The only thing we need more of is forgiveness, and Jesus already has satisfied that need. As we confess our sins and ask for forgiveness daily, we also can be certain that Jesus has taken all our sins to the cross. As we remember our Baptism, we rejoice that our sinful selves were washed clean in Jesus' blood and He has given us all we need—forgiveness and eternal life.

What role do money or possessions play in your life? Do the desires for certain things cause you to stumble in your "race of faith"? Are you spending so much time making money that your Christian walk is hindered? Who or what holds first place in your life?

sTRE T C H I N G oU T

Why do you think it was so hard for the rich man to do as Jesus asked?

What would you have the hardest time letting go of?

How do your desires for certain possessions or money get in the way of your faith and trust in God?

What needs to happen for a proper relationship with God to be restored?

RUNNING THE RACE:
CHALLENGE FOR WEEK 4

Rewrite your purpose statement, making desired revisions.

How did the Holy Spirit help you to live out your God-given purpose this week?

List anything that is hindering you as you seek to fulfill God's
purpose for your life.

Choose one thing that is tripping you up. Pray for Jesus to
free you from this tangle. Write a plan of action for
dealing with this particular problem in your race of
faith.

How did your life bring glory to God this week?

And let us run with perseverance
the race marked out for us.
(Hebrews 12:1)

Week 5 will focus on the crucial quality of perseverance necessary for those who wish to "finish the race." Sticking with our commitments and goals may be difficult. *Perseverance* means refusing to give up. It is the choice to continue, no matter what. The path on which we are to persevere is "the race marked out for us." We will look at the path Jesus has charted for us in week 6. He calls us to continue on the path under His guidance and direction. Through Baptism God has specially equipped us to finish the race.

WEEK 5

STICKING WITH IT

The Power of Perseverance

Have you noticed that life is more like a marathon than a sprint? In a sprint, the runners burst out of the starting blocks, run at full speed for a few seconds, and the race is over. In a marathon, a longer commitment is required. A marathon runner must find the determination to keep going over long periods of time and must persevere through pain, fatigue, and discouragement. This is true in life as well.

If you have watched a marathon, you know that some runners do not finish the race. For some, a lack of training takes its toll. Injury may stop others. Some give up when they grow tired and others when the pain becomes too great. There are those who lack inspiration, those who are short on commitment, and still others who decide that the goal is not worth the cost.

Perseverance is a crucial component if we are to run the race of faith to completion. This is the quality that Hebrews 12:1 talks about: "And let us run with perseverance the race marked out for us." Perseverance requires sacrifice, commitment, and the determination to keep going even during trying circumstances. In the passage you are about to read, you will see a powerful example of both sacrificial and creative perseverance.

> One day as [Jesus] was teaching, Pharisees and teachers of the law, who had come from every village of Galilee and from Judea and Jerusalem, were sitting there. And the power of the Lord was present for Him to heal the sick. Some men came carrying a paralytic on a mat and tried to take him into the house to lay him before Jesus. When they could not find a way to do this because of the crowd, they

went up on the roof and lowered him on his mat through the tiles into the middle of the crowd, right in front of Jesus.

When Jesus saw their faith, He said, "Friend, your sins are forgiven." ... He said to the paralyzed man, "I tell you, get up, take your mat and go home." Immediately he stood up in front of them, took what he had been lying on and went home praising God. (Luke 5:17-20, 24-25)

The friends described in this passage demonstrated tremendous persistence for the sake of the paralyzed man. The man couldn't walk, so they carried him. The task was more than one of them could handle alone, so they worked together. The crowds prevented them from reaching the door, so they climbed to the roof. The roof had no opening, so the men created an opening and lowered the man right in front of Jesus. They couldn't heal their friend, but they knew that Jesus could. They were not willing to give up until they had done all they could.

God uses our faith and our actions to affect others. We do not have the power to heal or to change others, but Jesus can be revealed through our words, actions, and love. We cannot always change our situations, but we can learn to look at other options. We can be people who drop out of the race when the road becomes rocky, or we can ask God to make us living examples of those who refuse to quit and persevere in the face of obstacles.

When others look at you, what do they see? Do they see you as someone who is willing to go the "extra mile" despite the cost? Do they see you as one who gives up when the path Jesus has laid out for us is filled with obstacles? Or do they see someone who consistently reflects God's creativity and strength? Are you a living example of one who perseveres?

sTRE T C H I N G oU T

What impresses you about the friends of the paralyzed man? Why were they so persistent?

If you had been the paralytic, how would you have felt?

Describe a time you persevered or sacrificed for the sake of someone else or a time you wish you would have.

Describe a situation in which you could use some help, creativity, or determination. How is God's power available to you?

The Power of Christ

Were you ever surprised or disappointed when something didn't work out the way you thought it should? Maybe you spent months training for a particular sport and found yourself cut from the team. Maybe you spent hours studying for a test and ended up with a rotten grade. Perhaps you put all kinds of effort into a relationship and the other person didn't seem to care. Or maybe you counted on a certain event to help you feel closer to God and it didn't happen.

In the Bible passage you are about to read, a group of professional fishermen came to shore after a long night of fishing. They had worked hard, using their time-tested skills, wisdom, and insight. They had done everything humanly possible to catch fish, yet they had come up empty-handed. They had failed to accomplish what they had set out to do. They had no fish to show for their efforts. They had no food to sell to customers. Facing all this disappointment, no one expected what happened next.

> One day as Jesus was standing by the Lake of Gennesaret, with the people crowding around Him and listening to the word of God, He saw at the water's edge two boats, left there by the fishermen, who were washing their nets. He got into one of the boats, the one belonging to Simon, and asked him to put out a little from shore. Then He sat down and taught the people from the boat.
>
> When He had finished speaking, He said to Simon, "Put out into deep water, and let down the nets for a catch."

Simon answered, "Master, we've worked hard all night and haven't caught anything. But because You say so, I will let down the nets."

When they had done so, they caught such a large number of fish that their nets began to break. So they signaled their partners in the other boat to come and help them, and they came and filled both boats so full that they began to sink.

When Simon Peter saw this, he fell at Jesus' knees and said, "Go away from me, Lord; I am a sinful man!" For he and all his companions were astonished at the catch of fish they had taken, and so were James and John, the sons of Zebedee, Simon's partners.

Then Jesus said to Simon, "Don't be afraid; from now on you will catch men." So they pulled their boats up on shore, left everything and followed Him. (Luke 5:1-11)

Did you notice what Simon Peter said? "Master, we've worked hard all night long and haven't caught anything." Have you found yourself saying something similar?

- "Jesus, I've worked so hard, and I have nothing to show for it."

- "Lord, I've tried to reach out to this person, and she keeps pushing me away."

- "Father, this is something I've succeeded at in the past, but this time even my best effort isn't enough."

Did you notice what Jesus did? He sent the fishermen back onto the lake even though they had already spent the entire night there. This time He went with them. These fishermen were not novices. They were skilled professionals. But Jesus sent them back to try again—at a time that made no sense to those who know fishing. When they returned, having obeyed Christ's command rather than relying on their own skill and insight, the results were overwhelming.

Most of us don't like coming up empty-handed. However, it is exactly during those meager times that we see Christ and His love in ways we never would otherwise. It is during those times that we recognize we are not limited to what is humanly possible. It is during those times that we have an opportunity to grow in our faithfulness to God and to use the Spirit-given power to persevere that is ours through faith in Christ.

Do you have situations or relationships that come up empty? Maybe God is calling you to return to these very places and relationships accompanied by Jesus. Jesus does not ask us to work alone. He accompanies us every step of the way.

What do you do when you come up empty-handed? Do you put your trust in your own skill and knowledge or in Christ? Are you willing to try again with Jesus at your side?

sTRE T C H I N G oU T

Describe a situation or relationship in which you have come up empty-handed.

How might God be using times of "emptiness" as opportunities to trust Christ in new ways?

Jesus asked Peter to do what didn't make sense. He asked Peter to go out again even after he had spent hours on a boat catching nothing. List examples of things Jesus may ask of us that don't seem to make sense.

WEEK 5: DAY 3

The Power of Prayer

Julie prayed that her relationship with her father would improve. Her father was not mean, but he was distant and spent little time with her. She longed to feel wanted and loved by him. Day after day she prayed. Sometimes it seemed that things were getting a little better, but then her father would pull away again. Julie began to wonder if God really heard her prayers. At times she even wondered if He cared.

As she continued to pray, Julie gradually became aware of some of the hurt and pain her father was carrying. She became more compassionate, although she saw very little change in him. She knew her father didn't believe in Jesus, and she prayed fervently that God would soften his heart. Julie asked Jesus to reflect His love through her own acts of care and kindness. Once in a while she saw a flicker of appreciation and thought that she might be getting through to her father.

Julie continued to pour her heart out before the Lord. She grew to see her father through Jesus' eyes. The relationship improved slightly but still had a long way to go. Because she looked so intently for the ways God might choose to work, Julie began to see that Jesus was indeed at work, both in her life and in the life of her father.

Sometimes we wonder if prayer really matters. We may pray without seeing the results we desire or without any visible sign that God is listening. We may grow weary when our petitions appear to go unanswered. Perhaps we feel abandoned because Jesus seems far away. There may be times that we struggle to pray at all.

The Bible tells us that prayer does indeed matter and that God desires our perseverance in petitioning Him. Pay close attention to the message Jesus shares with us in the following Bible passage:

> And [Jesus] said to them, "Suppose one of you has a friend, and you go to him at midnight and say to him, 'Friend, lend me three loaves of bread; for a friend of mine has arrived, and I have nothing to set before him.' And he answers from within, 'Do not bother me; the door has already been locked, and my children are with me in bed; I cannot get up and give you anything.' I tell you, even though he will not get up and give him anything because he is his friend, at least because of his persistence he will get up and give him whatever he needs.
>
> "So I say to you, Ask, and it will be given you; search, and you will find; knock, and the door will be opened for you. For everyone who asks receives, and

everyone who searches finds, and for everyone who knocks, the door will be opened." (Luke 11:5-10 NRSV)

These verses remind us that the Lord invites our persistent prayer; however, God answers according to His perfect wisdom and with the best timing. Sometimes we get exactly what we ask for, and we get it quickly. At other times, God's answer appears slow or even nonexistent. Just as the friend in this Bible passage refused to give up, we, too, are called to continue to ask, to search, and to knock.

Persevering in prayer is not about achieving results. It is not about changing God's will. As we continue to pray, the Holy Spirit helps us to see situations in new ways. Often what we ask for changes as we continue to pray and to seek God's will. Perseverance in prayer also keeps us looking diligently for Christ's answers, and we are more likely to be aware of the ways that God is at work in our lives and the lives of others.

How's your prayer life these days? When you are tired or discouraged, do you turn to the Lord in prayer? Do you thank God for the many ways He blesses you? Do you confess your sins, asking for His forgiveness? Do you pray for your family members and friends, even for your enemies? Do you join your prayers with others at church or Bible study? Are you committed to spending regular time with Jesus, talking with Him? Do you trust Him to give you what is best at the best time? Persevering in prayer is a crucial quality for those who desire to stay in the race and finish strong.

List your prayer requests below.

Ask the Holy Spirit to help you persevere in prayer over the next days and weeks. In the space below, jot down notes as you become aware of God's answers. Remember that the Lord sometimes answers in unexpected ways.

WEEK 5: DAY 4

The Power of Counting the Cost

It was the first day of practice, and Adam's head was spinning. Coach Davis had just laid out the expectations for those who wanted to play on the basketball team. Coach wanted to be sure that everyone was clear about what they were getting themselves into. Team members had to be dedicated to grueling practices to get themselves into top physical and mental condition. There would be mandatory curfews and restrictions on certain outside activities. They were expected to give their all in games, even when they were behind or discouraged.

Coach Davis reminded the team that they would be up against some stiff competition. He warned that they would face teams with great skill and strength and that opposing players might take some cheap shots. He set lofty goals and challenged the players to set their standards high. In a sense, the coach was challenging them to "count the cost" so they would have a better idea of what to expect. He wanted them to know about the challenges they would face so they could be prepared to meet those challenges with determination and strength.

Coach Davis wanted to inspire his players to set their standards high and to have ambitious goals. When they were tired or discouraged, he wanted them to remember that this was the price involved in achieving their goals. Coach also wanted them to realize that the price was worth it. He wanted to build a team that would persevere even when they felt like giving up.

The same is true in our race of faith. We "count the cost" so we will persevere in difficult times. Jesus warned His disciples that they would face opposition. He said:

> "If the world hates you, keep in mind that it hated Me first. ... If they persecuted Me, they will persecute you also. ... They will treat you this way because of My name, for they do not know the One who sent Me. ... All this I have told you so that you will not go astray. ... I have told you this, so that when the time comes you will remember that I warned you." (John 15:18, 20-21; 16:1, 4)

The ways of our world are often in direct opposition to the ways of God. Knowing the truth will help us stand strong when people criticize us for our faith or for the choices we make according to God's will. Knowing the potential consequences will give us strength when someone makes fun of our beliefs or when we feel like giving up. Knowing what to expect helps us persevere when we are lonely or discouraged or when someone takes a cheap shot.

Jesus "counted the cost" and persevered to the end. Even in the face of torture, pain, ridicule, and rejection, Jesus refused to give up. Knowing that the cross was coming soon, Jesus said: "Now My heart is troubled, and what shall I say? 'Father, save Me from this hour?' No, it was for this very reason I came to this hour" (John 12:27). Jesus knew clearly why He had come, and nothing could stop Him from taking our sins to the cross. Jesus was aware of the price to be paid, and He was willing to pay it. In Luke 9:51, we read: "When the days drew near for Him to be taken up, He set His face to go to Jerusalem" (NRSV).

Jesus did not promise that following Him would be easy, but He did promise it would be worth it. In Matthew 5:10–12, Jesus said:

> "Blessed are those who are persecuted because of righteousness, for theirs is the kingdom of heaven. Blessed are you when people insult you, persecute you and falsely say all kinds of evil against you because of Me. Rejoice and be glad, because great is your reward in heaven, for in the same way they persecuted the prophets who were before you."

Have you "counted the cost" of following Jesus? Are you prepared to persevere by the power of the Holy Spirit even when the going gets tough? Do you long to hear Jesus say, "Well done, good and faithful servant!" (Matthew 25:21)?

sTRETCHING ouT

For what things would you sacrifice?

Have you ever felt as though your Christian faith has "cost" you in some way? Explain.

You cannot bear the burdens of faith alone. How do worship, the Lord's Supper, and Bible study provide strength for your faith journey?

The Power of Promise

Promises are important. Trustworthy promises give us endurance and renewed strength. They bring light to our darkness and give us something strong to stand on during the stormy times of life. Promises give us hope for the future and the will to go on when we are tempted to give up.

Our heavenly Father has been making promises and keeping them since the beginning of time. God promised Abraham that he would be the father of many nations and David that he would be king of Israel. God promised a child to Abraham and Sarah. He promised Noah that He would never send another flood to destroy the earth, and He promised the world that He would send a Messiah. In these and other examples, God has shown not only that He is a promise maker, but also a promise keeper.

We can find strength to continue when we grab hold of the truth that God is faithful to all His promises. In

Hebrews 10:23, we read: "Let us hold unswervingly to the hope we profess, for He who promised is faithful." We have been given the gift and privilege of standing on the promises of the One who is utterly and completely trustworthy.

The apostle Paul, who endured great hardship and suffering for the sake of the Gospel, found strength in the promises of God. Paul found power in the knowledge that God loved us so much that He sent His only Son, Jesus, to take away all of our sins. Paul wrote:

> And we know that in all things God works for the good of those who love Him, who have been called according to His purpose. … If God is for us, who can be against us? He who did not spare His own Son, but gave Him up for us all—how will He not also, along with Him, graciously give us all things? … Who shall separate us from the love of Christ? Shall trouble or hardship or persecution or famine or nakedness or danger or sword? … No, in all these things we are more than conquerors through Him who loved us. For I am convinced that neither death nor life, neither angels nor demons, neither the present nor the future, nor any powers, neither height nor depth, nor anything else in all creation, will be able to separate us from the love of God that is in Christ Jesus our Lord. (Romans 8:28, 31-32, 35, 37-39)

Paul clung to the promises of God and persevered through great trials and obstacles. He knew that the power of God is infinitely more powerful than anything or anyone. Paul drew stamina and inspiration from the truth that we are created with a purpose and that nothing can separate us from the love of God in Christ Jesus.

We, too, can find the strength and the inspiration to persevere as the Holy Spirit keeps us connected to

God and His promises. No matter what happens, or how hopeless life can seem at times, the Holy Spirit will help us cling to the promise that Jesus will never leave us to run the race alone. In Matthew 28:20, Jesus declares, "surely I am with you always, to the very end of the age." Every time we go to Holy Communion His presence with us is made real.

We can find strength in the knowledge that our lives have purpose: "'For I know the plans I have for you', declares the LORD, 'plans to prosper you and not to harm you, plans to give you hope and a future'" (Jeremiah 29:11).

We can trust in God's faithfulness and find strength in His Word: "Do not let your hearts be troubled. Trust in God; trust also in Me. In My Father's house are many rooms; if it were not so, I would have told you. I am going there to prepare a place for you. And if I go and prepare a place for you, I will come back and take you to be with Me that you also may be where I am" (John 14:1–3).

As we hit the toughest challenges to our forward journey, may we always remember that "He who promised is faithful" (Hebrews 10:23).

sTRETCHING oUT

What part(s) of the Bible verses you read today were most meaningful? Why?

In what situation(s) today do you need to find strength in Christ's promises?

Look through your Bible for promises that are meaningful to you and write them below. If you're not sure where to look, start with some of these: Psalm 34:18; James 4:8; Isaiah 43:1-2; John 16:33; Isaiah 40:29; John 14:27; Proverbs 3:5-6; or Philippians 2:13. A topical Bible may be helpful. Check with your pastor, youth worker, parents, or at your church library for other helpful resources.

RUNNING THE RACE:
CHALLENGE FOR WEEK 5

Review your memorization of the first part of Hebrews 12:1: "Therefore, since we are surrounded by such a great cloud of witnesses, let us throw off everything that hinders and the sin that so easily entangles." Add the next part: "And let us run with perseverance the race marked out for us."

Rewrite your purpose statement, making desired revisions.

How has the Holy Spirit helped you to live out your God-given purpose this week?

In what area of your faith journey do you need to ask God for some perseverance right now?

List things you believe the Holy Spirit has given to help you persevere.

Think of those who may be struggling to move forward in their faith. Write down a way that you could encourage them, and do it.

How has God led you to live to His glory this week?

WEEK 5

SIGNS ALONG THE WAY

How's Your Love Life?

Just as runners rely on markers to chart their path and keep them on course, the Bible provides markers to keep us on track as well. As we live for God's glory, a crucial marker is our love—our loving response to what Jesus has done for us. John, the disciple who stressed Jesus' love for him, wrote about the importance of love.

> Dear friends, let us love one another, for love comes from God. Everyone who loves has been born of God and knows God. Whoever does not love does not know God, because God is love. This is how God showed His love among us: He sent His one and only Son into the world that we might live through Him. This is love: not that we loved God, but that He loved us and sent His Son as an atoning sacrifice for our sins. Dear friends, since God so loved us, we also ought to love one another. (1 John 4:7-11)

The Bible says that love is extremely important. If we act in its absence, all of our efforts are meaningless.

> If I speak in the tongues of men and of angels, but have not love, I am only a resounding gong or a clanging cymbal. If I have the gift of prophecy and can fathom all mysteries and all knowledge, and if I have a faith that can move mountains, but have not love, I am nothing. If I give all I possess to the poor and surrender my body to the flames, but have not love, I gain nothing. (1 Corinthians 13:1-3)

Not only does God remind us of the importance of loving others, He also teaches us what love is and how to live it. He supplies markers to show us whether we are traveling down the path of love. God directed Paul to define love this way:

> Love is patient, love is kind. It does not envy, it does not boast, it is not proud. It is not rude, it is not self-seeking, it is not easily angered, it keeps no record of wrongs. Love does not delight in evil but rejoices with the truth. It always protects, always trusts, always hopes, always perseveres. Love never fails. (1 Corinthians 13:4-8)

These qualities are our "signs along the way." "Love is *patient*" is the first sign. As we ponder and continue to run, the next sign reminds us that "love is *kind.*" We think back over the last several days, weeks, and months and into our view comes the next sign, "Love *does not envy,*" and the next, "Love *does not boast.*" As we continue to run, the markers keep appearing before us. Yet the ultimate marker of love was Jesus as He endured torture and death to forgive the very sinners who were responsible for His suffering.

The signs along the way provide a framework by which to measure our love against the definition of true love given by God. Are we loving with Jesus' love? What do our actions say about our hearts? Are loving qualities evident in our lives? Are we striving to grow, asking God to give us those qualities we lack?

sTRE T C H I N G oU T

On a scale of 1 to 10, rate yourself on each of the qualities listed in the verses you just read.

Patience

1	2	3	4	5	6	7	8	9	10

Needs improvement   I do this well

Kindness

1　2　3　4　5　6　7　8　9　10

Needs improvement　　　　　　　　　I do this well

Do Not Envy

1　2　3　4　5　6　7　8　9　10

Needs improvement　　　　　　　　　I do this well

Do Not Brag/Not Prideful

1　2　3　4　5　6　7　8　9　10

Needs improvement　　　　　　　　　I do this well

Not Rude

1　2　3　4　5　6　7　8　9　10

Needs improvement　　　　　　　　　I do this well

Not Self-Seeking

1　2　3　4　5　6　7　8　9　10

Needs improvement　　　　　　　　　I do this well

Not Easily Angered

1　2　3　4　5　6　7　8　9　10

Needs improvement　　　　　　　　　I do this well

Keep No Record of Wrongs (Don't Hold Grudges)

1　2　3　4　5　6　7　8　9　10

Needs improvement　　　　　　　　　I do this well

Do Not Delight in Evil; Rejoice in Truth

1   2   3   4   5   6   7   8   9   10

Needs improvement   I do this well

Protect (Loyal—Defend and Protect Others)

1   2   3   4   5   6   7   8   9   10

Needs improvement   I do this well

Trust

1   2   3   4   5   6   7   8   9   10

Needs improvement   I do this well

Hope

1   2   3   4   5   6   7   8   9   10

Needs improvement   I do this well

Perseverance

1   2   3   4   5   6   7   8   9   10

Needs improvement   I do this well

Choose one of the qualities in which you rated yourself on the low end and write it below. Pray for Jesus' help to make it a strength.

Love Is Patient and Kind

"Can I have a pencil?" the little voice squeaked.

Jim was trying to study for a test, and his little sister had asked for something every five minutes for the past hour. He was baby-sitting while his parents were at a meeting, but he needed to study too. Jackie's big blue eyes stared at him in anticipation. She was perfectly capable of getting her own pencil and most of the other things she had asked for. Jim had humored her at first, but his patience was wearing thin.

He clenched his teeth, took a deep breath, then noticed a tear running down his younger sister's cheek. "When will Mom and Dad be home?" she gulped, holding back more tears. She glanced outside at the dark sky, and suddenly Jim saw her fear and loneliness. She just wanted attention and reassurance that someone cared about her.

Some opportunities to love others come at inconvenient times. We can think of it as the "opportunity of interruptions." It is during these interruptions that our love is often put to the test. Our patience is stretched, and kindness is the last thing on our minds. The Bible, however, says that love is both patient and kind. These characteristics are "signs along our way" and a snapshot of the love for others that the Holy Spirit places in our hearts.

Jesus demonstrated remarkable patience and kindness in the most unexpected and inconvenient times, the most notable was when, despite His unimaginable, physical agony, He forgave those who made fun of Him (Luke 23:34). We find a powerful example of how Jesus responded to other interruptions in Luke 18:

> As Jesus approached Jericho, a blind man was sitting by the roadside begging. When he heard the crowd going by, he asked what was happening. They told him, "Jesus of Nazareth is passing by."
>
> He called out, "Jesus, Son of David, have mercy on me!"
>
> Those who led the way rebuked him and told him to be quiet, but he shouted all the more, "Son of David, have mercy on me!"
>
> Jesus stopped and ordered the man to be brought to Him. When he came near, Jesus asked him, "What do you want Me to do for you?"
>
> "Lord, I want to see," he replied.
>
> Jesus said to him, "Receive your sight; your faith has healed you." (Luke 18:35-42)

The crowd had a much different reaction to the blind man than Jesus did. The crowd was annoyed by his interruption. The text tells us they "rebuked him and told him to be quiet." Jesus, however, saw this interruption as an opportunity. He cared about the needs of this man who was crying out, and He responded with patience and kindness—and healing.

How do you respond when you are interrupted? Do you react in a way similar to those who surrounded the blind man in our passage? Do you view the interruptions of those in need as an annoyance, or do you see the interruptions as an opportunity to share Jesus' love through your patience and kindness? Can you see the need behind the cry and the opportunity behind the interruption?

sTRETCHING oUT

Describe a time you were interrupted and how you responded.

Who has shown you patience and/or kindness? How were you affected?

Why do you think God chose specifically to list patience and kindness as important qualities of love?

Describe one situation or relationship in which you could use more patience or kindness.

WEEK 6: DAY 3

Love Does Not Envy

Kami caught herself daydreaming again. *I wish I could be more like Lisa, she thought to herself. Lisa gets all the breaks. She's beautiful, smart, and talented. Her family has lots of money, and all the guys want to go out with her. It seems like everything goes right for her, and everything goes wrong for me. I wish I could look like Lisa. I wish I could be as smart as Lisa. I wish I could be as talented as Lisa. I wish I could be as popular as Lisa. I wish I could have all the nice things that Lisa has. It isn't fair that she gets everything. She should have to learn what it feels like to be ordinary like me!*

Kami began to speak negatively about Lisa. She began to gossip and spread rumors and say hurtful things behind Lisa's back. Kami was jealous, and her jealousy ate away at her integrity. She wanted what Lisa had and failed to recognize her own gifts and blessings from God.

Envy is a poison that kills love. When jealousy gets the best of us, it eats away at our attitudes. We begin to act in ways that are not loving at all. Instead of building others up, we tear them down. In the book of Acts, we see an example of what jealousy can do. Paul and Barnabas had been teaching people about Jesus' death and resurrection and the forgiveness He brings those who believe in Him. The religious leaders became envious of the crowd's response.

> When the congregation was dismissed, many of the Jews and devout converts to Judaism followed Paul and Barnabas, who talked with them and urged them to continue in the grace of God.
>
> On the next Sabbath almost the whole city gathered to hear the word of the Lord. When the Jews saw the crowds, they were filled with jealousy and talked abusively against what Paul was saying. ... The word of the Lord spread through the whole region. But the Jews incited the God-fearing women of high standing and the leading men of the city. They

stirred up persecution against Paul and Barnabas, and expelled them from their region. (Acts 13:43-45, 49-50)

Envy is a warning sign on the path of love. Envy often leads to other non-loving qualities. When we are jealous, we may try to build ourselves up by boasting or bragging. Like the Jews in the passage we just read, we become proud, rude, easily angered, and hold grudges because we feel threatened by the popularity or success of another. We want what others have, and we become self-seeking, me-oriented people. Scripture says that these qualities are not the qualities of real love: "[Love] does not envy, it does not boast, it is not proud. It is not rude, it is not self-seeking, it is not easily angered" (1 Corinthians 13:4-5).

Are you seeing some warning signs in your life? Are you so focused on what others have that you fail to see what God has given to you? Has envy slithered into your life and brought with it pride, rude behavior, or a hot temper? Are you focused on getting for yourself, or are you running the race of faith with humility and love?

sTRETCHING oUT

Describe any jealousy you have.

How does your envy affect your love for others?

Micah 6:8 says: "And what does the LORD require of you? To act justly and to love mercy and to walk humbly with your God." What do you think it means to "walk humbly with your God"? How does the Holy Spirit help you deal with jealousy?

WEEK 6: DAY 4

Love Protects

Tuesday started out like any other weekday morning. Students attended classes as usual, and, as usual, they laughed and talked, studied and discussed. It was just another day until two gunmen entered the school and began firing guns. School staff, as well as students, scrambled to rush potential victims to safety.

One teacher raced from room to room to warn people and direct them to take cover. In his race to protect others, Mr. Sanders was shot in the chest. Although he was severely wounded, he continued to warn and direct others. He eventually dragged himself into a classroom, joining a group of students who had taken cover. Hours later, Mr. Sanders died. He died because his love for others drove him to do all he could to protect them. His love reminds us of Jesus' love. Jesus sacrificed His life so we could live.

1 Corinthians 13:7 says that love "always protects." This teacher and other courageous and loving people demonstrated protective love on that tragic day. Sometimes protecting is costly. For Mr. Sanders, it cost him his life.

In response to Jesus' sacrificial love, God helps us to live with protective love. We may not be asked to give our lives, but people need our protective love in other ways. We may be in a position to put an end to rumors, gossip, or sarcasm that kills self-image. We may be asked to protect someone who is ridiculed, harassed, or bullied. Perhaps we can protect someone's confidentiality or privacy. God also may look to us to provide a covering of love for someone who is left out or lonely or to guard someone whose heart is tender.

Jesus demonstrated this protective kind of love again and again. God directed the apostle John to share this example:

> But Jesus went to the Mount of Olives. At dawn He appeared again in the temple courts, where all the people gathered around Him, and He sat down to teach them. The teachers of the law and the Pharisees brought in a woman caught in adultery. They made her stand before the group and said to Jesus, "Teacher, this woman was caught in the act of adultery. In the Law Moses commanded us to stone such women. Now what do you say?" They were using this question as a trap, in order to have a basis for accusing Him.
>
> But Jesus bent down and started to write on the ground with His finger. When they kept on questioning Him, He straightened up and said to them, "If any one of you is without sin, let him be the first to throw a stone at her." Again He stooped down and wrote on the ground.
>
> At this, those who heard began to go away one at a time, the older ones first, until only Jesus was left, with the woman still standing there. Jesus straight-

ened up and asked her, "Woman, where are they? Has no one condemned you?"

"No one, Sir," she said.

"Then neither do I condemn you," Jesus declared. "Go now and leave your life of sin." (John 8:1-11)

Real evidence of our love is shown in our actions and words. The religious leaders used their power and authority to attack. Jesus used His to protect. While Jesus did not condone the woman's adultery, His unconditional love moved Him to protect her from further shame and humiliation.

"Love protects" is an important "sign along the way" as we run our race of faith. It reminds us that real love defends, guards, and provides a place of refuge. Are you seeking God's guidance so you may practice this protective kind of love?

sTRETCHING ouT

How have you received "protective love" from God? From others?

Describe situations in which you see a need for someone to be protected.

In what situations will you ask the Holy Spirit to help you love with "protective love"?

WEEK 6: DAY 5
Love Trusts

Jeannie had tried for weeks to ride her bike without the training wheels. She would push off from the front steps of her house over and over, only to fall within a few feet. Her dad spent many hours watching, helping her get up again, and building her confidence. He knew that this was a big deal for his 5-year-old daughter. Finally, he suggested that they move away from the security of the steps and onto the sidewalk to give it a try.

"I know you can do it," Jeannie's father urged. Then he promised to hold the seat until she was balancing on her own. With the cheers and confidence of her dad, the little girl was off down the street on the first try, excited that she could ride and balance all on her own!

How important it is to have people who love us, who believe in us, and who let us go! It is in being loved and "let go" that we use God's gifts and talents. The Bible reminds us that love "believes all things" (1 Corinthians 13:7 NRSV). If we read the whole verse, we see just how important and powerful love is: "[Love] bears all things, believes all things, hopes all things, and endures all things."

People experience true love when they know that someone has confidence in them and expects the best of them. There are many in our world who desperately need this kind of encouragement to gain the confidence and inspiration to use the many gifts God has given them. God has given you the power to trust and to be trusted. He created this condition when He sent Jesus to forgive you and the Holy Spirit to nurture faith in you.

There are many who have been intensely inspired because someone had confidence in them. Hundreds of years ago a young man known as John Mark was profoundly affected by an older man named Barnabas who believed in him. John Mark had joined Barnabas and the apostle Paul on their first missionary journey, but for some reason he returned home without completing the mission. Paul was angry with his decision. The story continues:

> Some time later Paul said to Barnabas, "Let us go back and visit the brothers in all the towns where we preached the word of the Lord and see how they are doing." Barnabas wanted to take John, also called Mark, with them, but Paul did not think it wise to take him, because he had deserted them in Pamphylia and had not continued with them in the work. They had such a sharp disagreement that they parted company. Barnabas took Mark and sailed for Cyprus. (Acts 15:36-39)

Barnabas gave John Mark another chance. He was willing to show John Mark trust and confidence. Through the encouragement of Barnabas, John Mark eventually became a great influence on the early church. He was inspired to write the book of Mark in the Bible. He was later reunited with Paul and became a valued friend of this older apostle. It was this trusting kind of love that made a difference in the life of John Mark.

This sign along the way reads: "Love trusts." To whom can you show trusting love? Who could use the encouragement of knowing that you believe in them?

sTRE T C H I N G oUT

Name someone who trusts you.

How can you show people that you have confidence in them?

How has Jesus trusted you? How does the Holy Spirit help
you to trust?

RUNNING THE RACE:
CHALLENGE FOR WEEK 6

Rewrite your purpose statement, making desired revisions.

How has the Holy Spirit helped you to live out your God-given
purpose this week?

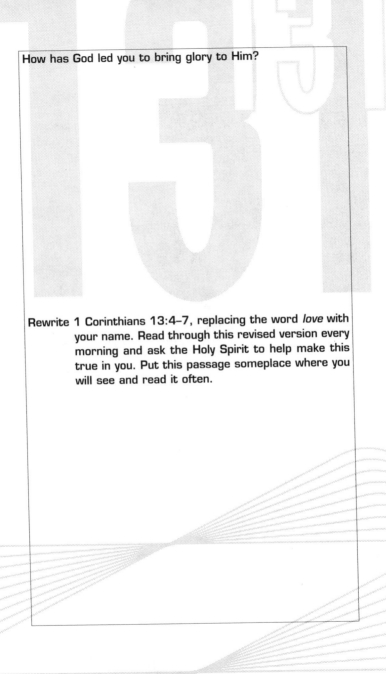

How has God led you to bring glory to Him?

Rewrite 1 Corinthians 13:4–7, replacing the word *love* with your name. Read through this revised version every morning and ask the Holy Spirit to help make this true in you. Put this passage someplace where you will see and read it often.

Let us fix our eyes on Jesus, the
author and perfecter of our faith,
who for the joy set before Him
endured the cross, scorning its
shame, and sat down at the right
hand of the throne of God.
(Hebrews 12:2)

Week 7 will challenge you to look seriously at how you focus on others. With our eyes focused on Jesus, all of life takes on a new perspective. Through eyes of love, He urges us onward. We see Jesus enduring the cross on our behalf. The picture of love that Jesus paints is one that includes all Christians living out the purpose for which they were created. In the final week, you will be challenged to create a spiritual training plan to help you become more intentional in your race of faith. Living in faithfulness doesn't just happen. It is a process blessed and enabled by the Holy Spirit with Jesus leading the way.

WEEK 7

FIXING OUR EYES

ON JESUS

Jesus up Close

There she was again. Jeff tried not to stare, but he couldn't stop himself. Kate was the most beautiful girl he had ever seen. Her long blonde hair shimmered like sunshine, and her deep blue eyes just about made him melt. He had memorized the way she walked and could see her warm smile and the kindness of her face even with his eyes closed.

The more he watched her, the more he could read her moods by the expression on her face or by the way she walked. He knew when she was discouraged or disappointed, as well as when she was playful and happy. Jeff could tell in which of her friends she confided most and which situations appeared to frustrate her. In time, he could predict how she would respond to certain situations. He could see the compassion in her eyes as she comforted a classmate or encouraged someone who was down. He could still picture her sincerity when she had thanked him for helping her with a geography assignment.

There is a difference between merely looking at someone and truly "seeing" them. Hebrews 12:2 reminds us of the importance of seeing Jesus: "Let us fix our eyes on Jesus." When we fix our eyes on Jesus, we see things we can't see when we take a quick glance. We understand more about what is important to Him. When we fix our eyes on Jesus, we see Him through the eyes of faith, and, in the process, we want to be more like Him. Mary, a close friend of Jesus, was a wonderful example of one who fixed her eyes on Jesus.

> As Jesus and His disciples were on their way, He came to a village where a woman named Martha opened her home to Him. She had a sister called

> Mary, who sat at the Lord's feet listening to what He said. But Martha was distracted by all the preparations that had to be made. She came to Him and asked, "Lord, don't You care that my sister has left me to do the work by myself? Tell her to help me!"
>
> "Martha, Martha," the Lord answered, "you are worried and upset about many things, but only one thing is needed. Mary has chosen what is better, and it will not be taken away from her." (Luke 10:38-42)

Mary had a different perspective because she had "fixed her eyes on Jesus." Jesus said, "Mary has chosen what is better." She had studied her Lord and loved Him deeply and wanted to learn from Him. By the power of the Holy Spirit, Mary focused on Jesus and grew in her knowledge and understanding of Him. We later read about her coming to Jesus shortly before His death and anointing Him with expensive perfume. While the disciples scoffed at her seemingly wasteful gesture, Jesus praised her actions, saying: "When she poured this perfume on My body, she did it to prepare Me for burial. I tell you the truth, wherever this gospel is preached throughout the world, what she has done will also be told, in memory of her" (Matthew 26:12-13). Mary saw what the disciples didn't. She saw Jesus as the one who loved her as no one else could. In return, she loved and cherished Him.

Have you taken the time to fix your eyes on Jesus? Have you studied His image in Scripture? Have you sat at His feet in worship? Have you come into the presence of His body and blood at the Lord's Table? How does God's Word give you insight into His character? Jesus is waiting to be seen.

STRETCHING OUT

Are you more like Mary or Martha? Explain.

Describe your image of Jesus and where that image comes from.

What might help you see Jesus more clearly?

WEEK 7: DAY 2

Jesus in the Distance

As Carl headed down the street for his daily run, soft snowflakes began to fall. Gray clouds loomed overhead, but Carl liked running through the cool fresh snow. When he was several miles from home, the snow began to fall more heavily. Before he knew it, Carl found himself in a blinding blizzard. He turned toward home, only to realize that his path was completely covered by snow. He couldn't see more than a few feet ahead. He continued to run in what he hoped was the right direction. After several minutes, Carl saw a faint light in the distance. He recognized it as a street light on a familiar street that would lead him home. He knew that he would be okay if he just kept his eyes focused on the light ahead rather than on the blizzard that surrounded him.

In the passage you are about to read, one of Jesus' disciples, Peter, learns a powerful lesson about maintaining focus.

Immediately Jesus made the disciples get into the boat and go on ahead of Him to the other side, while He dismissed the crowd. After He had dismissed them, He went up on a mountainside by Himself to pray. When evening came, He was there alone, but the boat was already a considerable distance from land, buffeted by the waves because the wind was against it.

During the fourth watch of the night Jesus went out to them, walking on the lake. When the disciples saw Him walking on the lake, they were terrified. "It's a ghost," they said, and cried out in fear.

But Jesus immediately said to them: "Take courage! It is I. Don't be afraid."

"Lord, if it's You," Peter replied, "tell me to come to You on the water."

"Come," He said.

Then Peter got down out of the boat, walked on the water and came toward Jesus. But when he saw the wind, he was afraid and, beginning to sink, cried out, "Lord, save me!"

Immediately Jesus reached out His hand and caught him. "You of little faith," He said, "why did you doubt?"

> And when they climbed into the boat, the wind died down. Then those who were in the boat worshiped Him, saying, "Truly You are the Son of God." (Matthew 14:22-33)

This story illustrates the difference it makes when Jesus is the focus instead of worldly concerns. Peter did fine as long as he kept his eyes on Jesus. When he "saw the wind" and noticed the waves, Peter focused on the impossibility of what he was doing. Filled with doubt, Peter began to sink. The same is true for us. When we take our eyes off Jesus and get lost in the winds of fear and the waves of problems, we sink into discouragement and hopelessness. When our focus remains on Christ, our trust in God holds firm. When we lose sight of Jesus hanging on the cross and fix our eyes on our own attempts at salvation, we can't see Jesus at all.

When the Holy Spirit fixes our eyes on Jesus, our entire perspective is changed, and we are empowered to live for Him. Worship, regular study of God's Word, and faithful trips to the Lord's Table, keep us focused on Jesus as we run our race of faith.

Where do you fix your eyes? Do you focus on your struggles or the parts of life that seem unfair? Do you spend too much time staring at the obstacles and the uncertainties of life? Do you become overwhelmed by your situations, or do you fix your eyes on Jesus?

sTRETCHING ouT

Why do you think Jesus invited Peter to step out of the boat?

What are some "winds" or "waves" in your life?

On what are you more focused—Jesus or the "wind" and
"waves"?

How would life be different if your eyes remained focused on
Jesus?

How do your eyes become focused on Jesus?

WEEK 7: DAY 3

Jesus on the Cross

We don't like to see people in pain. It's hard to
see people suffer. Jesus endured great pain on our
behalf. It is important that we see His suffering to
remember the kind of God we serve and the hope that is
ours through Him. Hebrews 12:2 says, "Let us fix our
eyes on Jesus, the author and perfecter of our faith, who
for the joy set before Him endured the cross, scorning its
shame, and sat down at the right hand of the throne of

God." We need to look closely at the moments leading to Jesus' crucifixion so we might see the ultimate picture of love.

> Then the governor's soldiers took Jesus into the Praetorium and gathered the whole company of soldiers around Him. They stripped Him and put a scarlet robe on Him, and then twisted together a crown of thorns and set it on His head. They put a staff in His right hand and knelt in front of Him and mocked Him. "Hail, king of the Jews!" they said. They spit on Him, and took the staff and struck Him on the head again and again. After they had mocked Him, they took off the robe and put His own clothes on Him. Then they led Him away to crucify Him. (Matthew 27:27-31)

Crucifixion was a common Roman penalty and was the cruelest death possible. The criminal was stripped, and his hands were tied behind his back. He was lashed over and over with a long leather thong embedded with sharp pieces of bone and pellets of lead. Eventually the criminal's skin would hang in long strips of tissue, and the entire area would become an ugly mass of torn, bleeding flesh. The beating would finally stop when the prisoner was near death. The criminal then would be forced to carry his cross to the place where he would die. A soldier would walk ahead of the one sentenced to death, carrying a sign that spelled out the crime. Finally, the prisoner was fastened to the cross and left to die.

Jesus not only endured great physical pain, He also was inflicted with stinging insults and shame-filled accusations.

> Two robbers were crucified with Him, one on His right and one on His left. Those who passed by hurled insults at Him, shaking their heads and saying,

"You who are going to destroy the temple and build it in three days, save Yourself! Come down from the cross, if You are the Son of God!"

In the same way the chief priests, the teachers of the law and the elders mocked Him. "He saved others," they said, "but He can't save Himself! He's the King of Israel! Let Him come down now from the cross, and we will believe in Him. He trusts in God. Let God rescue Him now if He wants Him, for He said, 'I am the Son of God.'" In the same way the robbers who were crucified with Him also heaped insults on Him.

From the sixth hour until the ninth hour darkness came over all the land. About the ninth hour Jesus cried out in a loud voice, "Eloi, Eloi, lama sabachthani?"—which means, "My God, My God, why have You forsaken Me?" (Matthew 27:38-46)

When He had received the drink, Jesus said, "It is finished." With that, He bowed His head and gave up His spirit." (John 19:30)

Jesus called out with a loud voice, "Father, into Your hands I commit My spirit." When He had said this, He breathed His last. (Luke 23:46)

When we fix our eyes on Jesus, we see God on a cross. We see a thorny crown ripping wounds in His skull, and blood trickling down His bruised and swollen face. We picture our sinless Savior, labeled a criminal, mocked and ridiculed as His hands and feet are pierced with nails. There is agony in His eyes as He writhes in pain and struggles to breathe. He is lonely and abandoned, the innocent victim of our sins. When we fix our eyes on Jesus, we see a Savior who loved us so much that He endured persecution and death to take away our sins and give us new life.

When you see a picture of Christ on the cross in your heart and mind, what thoughts and feelings do you experience? Does this picture cause gratitude? Does it inspire you to run each step of your race with faithfulness and determination? Does it deepen your love for Jesus?

sTRE T C H I N G oU T

What thoughts and feelings does Jesus' crucifixion raise in you?

Write a letter to Jesus, expressing your thoughts and feelings regarding His death on your behalf.

Jesus in Our Midst

It was her little brother's favorite game, and Kelly found herself once again searching for the right spot. Hide-and-seek was a daily ritual that took place the moment Kelly was excitedly welcomed home by Mike. It was Kelly's turn to hide, and as Mike counted, Kelly quickly climbed a large tree in the backyard. She thought that Mike would find her in no time, but she knew that her little brother would laugh long and hard when he discovered her hunched within the tree branches.

Mike had finished counting and enthusiastically began searching. He flung open the garage door, shuffled through a huge pile of leaves, checked behind the bushes, and peered over the fence. Several times he walked directly beneath Kelly, but not once did he look up. Mike was so close that he could have reached up and touched her, but he was completely unaware of how close he really was. It wasn't until Kelly threw acorns at him that Mike finally thought to look up.

Sometimes we do the same thing in our faith relationship with Jesus. We get "stuck" in a certain mindset or way of looking at things, and we miss seeing Jesus even though He is with us always. In the story we are about to read, two of Jesus' disciples had lost sight of Him and needed to have their eyes opened. When this story took place, Jesus had risen from the dead and the news had just begun to spread through Jerusalem. Listen carefully for this passage's message.

Now that same day two of them were going to a village called Emmaus, about seven miles from Jerusalem. They were talking with each other about everything that had happened. As they talked and discussed these things with each other, Jesus Himself came up and walked along with them; but they were kept from recognizing Him.

He asked them, "What are you discussing together as you walk along?"

They stood still, their faces downcast. One of them, named Cleopas, asked Him, "Are you only a visitor to Jerusalem and do not know the things that have happened there in these days?"

"What things?" He asked.

"About Jesus of Nazareth," they replied. "He was a prophet, powerful in word and deed before God and all people. The chief priests and our rulers handed Him over to be sentenced to death, and they crucified Him; but we had hoped that He was the one who was going to redeem Israel. And what is more, it is the third day since all this took place. In addition, some of our women amazed us. They went to the tomb early this morning but didn't find His body. They came and told us that they had seen a vision of angels, who said He was alive. Then some of our companions went to the tomb and found it just as the women had said, but Him they did not see."

[Jesus] said to them, " ... Did not the Christ have to suffer these things and then enter His glory?" And beginning with Moses and all the Prophets, He explained to them what was said in all the Scriptures concerning Himself.

As they approached the village to which they were going, Jesus acted as if He were going farther. But they urged Him strongly, "Stay with us, for it is nearly evening; the day is almost over." So He went in to stay with them.

When He was at the table with them, He took bread, gave thanks, broke it and began to give it to them. Then their eyes were opened and they recognized Him, and He disappeared from their sight. (Luke 24:13-31)

Disappointment can cloud our vision. These disciples had trusted Jesus to deliver them from the rulers of their day. They thought that Jesus had been defeated on the cross. Their hope had been shattered. The disciples' minds were so focused on their loss that they could not see the reality of Christ's presence.

Jesus opened their eyes and their minds to see Him through the words of Scripture. He pointed out that His death was not an accident and that God had planned the events of Jesus' life, death, and resurrection. Jesus reminded them of their history, of the promises of Scripture, and of God's faithfulness.

We, too, see the risen Christ. Jesus suffered death on the cross, but the Gospel message proclaims that Jesus was raised from the dead. The tomb is empty. Jesus is alive and is present with us. He seeks us out and makes Himself known to us by the power of the Holy Spirit working through the Bible, Baptism, and Holy Communion. We serve a living Lord.

sTRE T C H I N G oU T

How do you think the men felt when they recognized Jesus?

What does God do to get your attention?

What did you learn about how our eyes are opened to the truth about Jesus?

How does this story give you hope?

Jesus on the Throne

Not only do we see the risen Christ, we also can envision Jesus in heaven. Hebrews 12:2 tells us that Jesus "sat down at the right hand of the throne of God." Jesus is the God of both heaven and earth. Life is not limited to earth. For those who follow Jesus, there is the promise of eternal life with Him. In John 3:16, we read, "For God so loved the world that He gave His one and only Son, that whoever believes in Him shall not perish but have eternal life." When the Holy Spirit fixes our eyes on Jesus, we see a glimpse of the life that awaits us, and we run our race with that in mind.

People with limited vision cannot see clearly; however, their lack of clear vision does not make what they cannot see any less real. Like a person with limited vision, we see only a blurred image of what awaits us in heaven. Our inability to see clearly does not make heaven any less real, however, because we know that God's Word is faithful and true. Jesus promised: "In My Father's house are many rooms; if it were not so, I would have told you. I am going there to prepare a place for you. And if I go and prepare a place for you, I will come back and take you to be with Me that you also may be where I am" (John 14:2–3). And in 1 Corinthians 13:12, we read: "Now we see but a poor reflection as in a mirror; then we shall see face to face."

In the book of Revelation, we read of a vision that God gave to the apostle John. God gives us a peek at the heavenly scene that awaits us:

On the Lord's Day I was in the Spirit, and I heard behind me a loud voice like a trumpet ... I turned around to see the voice that was speaking to me. And when I turned I saw ... someone "like a Son of Man," dressed in a robe reaching down to His feet and with a golden sash around His chest. His head and hair were white like wool, as white as snow, and His eyes were like blazing fire. His feet were like bronze glowing in a furnace, and His voice was like the sound of rushing waters ... and out of His mouth came a sharp double-edged sword. His face was like the sun shining in all its brilliance. When I saw Him, I fell at His feet as though dead. Then He placed His right hand on me and said: "Do not be afraid. I am the First and the Last. I am the Living One; I was dead, and behold I am alive for ever and ever!" (Revelation 1:10, 12-18)

After this I looked, and there before me was a door standing open in heaven. And the voice I had first heard speaking to me like a trumpet said, "Come up here, and I will show you what must take place after this." At once I was in the Spirit, and there before me was a throne in heaven with someone sitting on it. And the one who sat there had the appearance of jasper and carnelian. A rainbow, resembling an emerald, encircled the throne. ... From the throne came flashes of lightning, rumblings and peals of thunder. Before the throne, seven lamps were blazing. These are the seven spirits of God. Also before the throne there was what looked like a sea of glass, clear as crystal. (Revelation 4:1-3, 5-6)

And I heard a loud voice from the throne saying, "Now the dwelling of God is with men, and He will live with them. They will be His people, and God Himself will be with them and be their God. He will wipe every tear from their eyes. There will be no more death or mourning or crying or pain, for the old order of things has passed away." (Revelation 21:3-4)

As we fix our eyes on Jesus and see Him sitting beside the throne of God, we begin to see beyond the horizon of this world and into eternity. In the promise of heaven, we find true and lasting hope. It brings renewed purpose to the race. It is in this image of Christ at the throne of God that we remember we serve a loving, righteous, eternal, and all-powerful God. Are you ready to stand before the Creator of the Universe and see your Savior face-to-face?

sTRETCHING oUT

What thoughts and feelings do you have when you think of seeing Jesus face-to-face?

Why is it helpful to picture Jesus sitting at the right hand of God's throne?

After reading today's Bible verses or others that you know, do you see yourself in this picture of heaven? Why?

RUNNING THE RACE:
CHALLENGE FOR WEEK 7

Review your memorization of Hebrews 12:1: "Therefore,
        since we are surrounded by such a great cloud of
        witnesses, let us throw off everything that hinders
        and the sin that so easily entangles, and let us run
        with perseverance the race marked out for us."
        Then memorize Hebrews 12:2: "Let us fix our eyes
        on Jesus, the author and perfecter of our faith,
        who for the joy set before Him endured the cross,
        scorning its shame, and sat down at the right hand
        of the throne of God."

Rewrite your purpose statement, making desired revisions.

How has the Holy Spirit helped you to live out your God-given
        purpose this week?

Draw a picture or create a collage of what you see when you fix your eyes on Jesus.

How has the Holy Spirit led you to live to God's glory this week?

In 1 John 4:12, we read: "No one has ever seen God; but if we love one another, God lives in us and His love is made complete in us." Ask the Holy Spirit to help you fix your eyes on Jesus today. As you focus on Him, ask the Holy Spirit to work in your life so others might see Jesus in you.

WEEK 8

THE TRAINING PLAN

By His Spirit

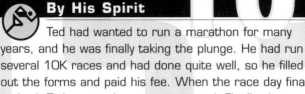

Ted had wanted to run a marathon for many years, and he was finally taking the plunge. He had run several 10K races and had done quite well, so he filled out the forms and paid his fee. When the race day finally arrived, Ted was anxious to get started. Finally, the starter called Ted's name, and the race began. At the 12-mile mark, Ted had trouble breathing. A mile later, his legs cramped, and he dropped out of the race. Ted had tried, but sadly, Ted hadn't trained.

Dave, on the other hand, had trained faithfully and diligently. He had carved time out of his schedule for training and stuck with his commitment. He lifted weights to strengthen his muscles, ate a healthy diet, and balanced running with other forms of exercise. The more he trained, the stronger he became. Although there were many days he forced himself to run when he didn't feel like it, his body gradually began to desire and even crave running. Dave ran the same race as Ted, and even though he stumbled occasionally and experienced pain and fatigue, he finished the race and accomplished his goal.

Trying is important, but without training we can't go the distance. Just as marathon runners need to train and condition their bodies and minds, we, too, need to train spiritually so we can make a strong finish in our race of faith. The apostle Paul shares these wise words regarding the need for training: "Train yourself to be godly. For physical training is of some value, but godliness has value for all things, holding promise for both the present life and the life to come" (1 Timothy 4:7b–8).

The race of faith is a lifelong race that requires discipline and commitment. It is a race that may cost us greatly, but it is rewarding for all eternity. The apostle Paul knew firsthand the cost of following Jesus. He also knew the reward. Paul writes: "Athletes exercise self-control in all things; they do it to receive a perishable wreath, but we an imperishable one" (1 Corinthians 9:25 NRSV).

Do not be discouraged. Jesus took the pain that we could not tolerate. He overcame the obstacles that would have kept us from completing the race. Now we run in faith. Whatever we give up is nothing compared to what Jesus already has given up to win our salvation.

As a part of these last five devotions, you will have the opportunity to create a spiritual training plan. Whether you know it or not, God has inspired and stretched you as you have studied the thoughts and Scripture passages in this book. As you near the end of this book, the race is really beginning. While learning is important, the key is to put what we learn into practice. Like an athlete training for an event, a spiritual training plan tapped into the power of the Holy Spirit will help us run the race of faith to completion.

A spiritual training plan is "spiritual" only as it is guided and directed by the Spirit of God. Therefore, that is where we begin. In Zechariah 4:6, God gives us this important standard when He says, "Not by might nor by power, but by My Spirit." The Holy Spirit is our guide both in creating the training plan and in carrying it out.

In John 14:26, Jesus promised the Holy Spirit to the disciples and to us: "But the Counselor, the Holy Spirit, whom the Father will send in My name, will teach you all things and will remind you of everything I have said to you." The Holy Spirit speaks to our hearts, convinces our minds, and guides our souls.

sTRETCHING oUT

Write a prayer to God, asking Him to help you walk by His
Spirit.

Quiet Time

If we want to develop a close friendship with
someone, we spend time with that person regularly. The
same is true in our faith relationship with Jesus. A key
piece of our spiritual training plan is time with the Lord.
Obviously, we spend time with Jesus as we worship Him
and as we take part in the Lord's Supper. But we also
grow closer to Jesus as we spend time alone with Him—
talking, listening, thanking, praising, asking for help, offering our service, learning about Him, and enjoying His
company.

Just as runners sometimes crave running and at
other times must discipline themselves to run, we may
have similar feelings regarding our time with the Lord.
Jesus always wants to spend time with us. At times, you
may long to be with Him as well. At other times, you may
need to discipline yourself. That's why commitment is
important.

For many people, setting aside a regular time
each day helps to ensure that their quiet time doesn't get
squeezed out by a busy schedule. This does not mean
that you forget about the Lord the rest of the day. Jesus'

desire is to be a part of our every moment and to walk with us through each situation of life. Setting aside a regular time to be with the Lord helps us to give Him our focused attention. It is in this time that we understand an important benefit of our faith: "Come near to God and He will come near to you" (James 4:8).

The Holy Spirit draws us closer to Jesus as we spend time in His Word. In Scripture, God reveals Himself. Scripture shows how God fulfilled His promise of salvation through Jesus Christ.

Imagine for a moment that you have a friend you care about deeply. You want your friend to know you and to know the love you hold for him. You pour out your heart in one letter after another. How would you feel if your friend chose not to read your letters or only briefly skimmed them? The Bible is God's love letter to His people. In it, He pours out His heart and reveals His character and plans. As we study His Word, the Holy Spirit deepens and strengthens our faith in God.

Prayer also is an essential component of our quiet time with the Lord. God promises to reveal Himself to us as we seek Him in prayer: "'For I know the plans I have for you,' declares the LORD, 'plans to prosper you and not to harm you, plans to give you hope and a future. Then you will call upon Me and come and pray to Me, and I will listen to you. You will seek Me and find Me when you seek Me with all your heart. I will be found by you,' declares the LORD" (Jeremiah 29:11–14). God promises that He hears our prayers and that He is present for us. He is not a distant God, but a God who loves us perfectly.

As we pray, we spend time both sharing with the Lord and listening to Him. As in any other relationship, if we do all the talking, we miss benefiting from what the other person has to share. In John 10:27, Jesus says,

"My sheep listen to My voice; I know them, and they follow Me." Praying also involves hearing what God has to say in His Word. Whatever we pray about has an answer. We can discover that answer by searching Scripture and asking for the Holy Spirit's guidance.

While there are many different ways to go about your quiet time, one common and necessary element of quiet time is being intentional. It is wise to create a committed plan for spending time alone with the Lord. Determine a time and a place. Be sure you are spending some of your time reading Scripture. Some suggestions for your quiet time include: using a devotional with Scripture verses, reading through a particular book of the Bible, or looking up certain topics in a topical Bible. You may want to keep a journal such as the one you have kept in this book. Be sure to spend time in prayer. Many people find it helpful to begin their devotions with prayer, asking the Holy Spirit to open their hearts and minds to what He would choose to reveal through God's Word. You may end your quiet time with prayer as well.

By the power of the Holy Spirit, a commitment to daily quiet time will strengthen and reward you as you seek to run your race of faith. Through Baptism into Jesus' death and resurrection, you were recreated to live as God's beloved child and to experience the joy of being drawn close to Him.

sTRE T C H I N G oU T

Describe what you are currently doing for quiet time with Jesus.

If you do not have a regular quiet time with God, think of times and places that might work.

List resources you could study from or someone you could talk to for ideas.

Describe your prayer life and any improvements you would like to make. Pray for the Spirit's guidance as you do this.

WEEK 8: DAY 3
Worship and Group Participation

Just as there is a part of our faith relationship with Jesus that can be experienced in time alone with

Him, there is another part that can be experienced as we gather with other Christians. God created us to live in relationship with other believers. Our next level of commitment, therefore, involves both regular worship and participation in the Lord's Supper, as well as participation in some type of Christian group.

Worship offers an opportunity to praise God, learn more about Him through His Word, be strengthened by Him in Communion, and pray in the company of other believers. As we worship with others, we remember that we are a part of a larger community of faith. We can experience the common bond in the Lord. As we come together to worship the Lord, we bring Him glory through the power of the Holy Spirit. In Psalm 86:9, we read, "All the nations You have made will come and worship before You, O Lord; they will bring glory to Your name." Farther along in the psalms, we read: "Exalt the LORD our God and worship at His holy mountain, for the LORD our God is holy" (Psalm 99:9).

Worship not only brings honor to God, but as we worship, God is coming to us in His Word and sacraments. Worship offers an opportunity to hear words and ideas that stretch us. We find new things for which to praise God. We may be challenged to confront parts of our lives that have strayed off the path, or we may be touched with new compassion and understanding toward the needs of others. At other times, we may receive some much needed words of encouragement, healing, guidance, or insight. We always need to hear how Jesus took away our sins and gave us new life!

In addition to worshiping regularly, we can participate in some type of group that provides an opportunity to grow in our Christian faith. It is in conversation and relationship with others that we learn from each other, challenge each other, and build each other up in Christ. In Colossians 3:16–17, we are encouraged to join together with other believers:

> Let the word of Christ dwell in you richly as you teach and admonish one another with all wisdom, and as you sing psalms, hymns and spiritual songs with gratitude in your hearts to God. And whatever you do, whether in word or deed, do it all in the name of the Lord Jesus, giving thanks to God the Father through Him.

As these verses remind us, it is important that whatever we do, we do it "in the name of the Lord Jesus." As we interact with others, we learn to see from new perspectives, and we draw strength and comfort from the experiences of others.

Are you committed to worshiping in the community of faith on a regular basis? Do you participate in worship with a heart open to God? Do you frequently participate in Communion, asking for forgiveness, peace, and strength?

Do you participate in a Christian group? If so, do you "do it all in the name of the Lord Jesus, giving thanks to God the Father"? If not, is there such a group you could be a part of? Do you need to pray for God to lead you to a group or to start one of your own? Are you seeking the Lord in the community of faith and striving to grow through interaction with the body of believers?

sTRETCHING oUT

How have you worshiped the Lord in the past?

Describe the ways you currently worship.

What importance does the Lord's Supper have in your worship life?

Describe a Christian group that influenced you in the past.

Describe a Christian group that you are a part of or could be a part of.

Describe ideas for a Christian group you could start, or list some people you could talk to about finding a group.

Giving and Serving

We have talked about seeking Christ's guidance through the Holy Spirit, about spending time alone with the Lord in study of His Word and in prayer, about committing ourselves to worship and participation in a Christian group. Now we can talk about putting our faith into action. If we seek to grow in faith yet our faith is not put into practice, we have missed the whole point. We give of what we have because God has given us *everything* we have, including everything we need to live forever. In gratitude to God, Christians share their blessings and talents with the rest of the world.

The Bible speaks clearly about the importance of placing actions behind our words. In James 2:14–17, we read:

> What good is it, my brothers, if a man claims to have faith but has no deeds? Can such faith save him? Suppose a brother or sister is without clothes and daily food. If one of you says to him, "Go, I wish you well; keep warm and well fed," but does nothing about his physical needs, what good is it? In the same way, faith by itself, if it is not accompanied by action, is dead.

God calls us to a living faith; therefore, a part of our spiritual training includes a commitment to give and to serve. We will examine giving and serving from three different and equally important aspects: time, talent, and money. Through His Word, God calls us to share with others in each of these three areas and to be disciplined in our commitment to do so. As the Holy Spirit continues to strengthen our faith in Jesus, we give of ourselves for the sake of our loving Savior. This becomes a cycle in our lives: Our faith deepens and our desire to respond to this wonderful gift deepens as well.

That we offer our talents through service in Christ's name is our response to what Christ has done for us. Each of us has been given talents and abilities to serve the Lord. It is exciting to discover and use our abilities and gifts. What is even more exciting is finding places to share these talents with others.

Just as each of us has one body with many members, and these members do not all have the same function, so in Christ we who are many form one body, and each member belongs to all the others. We have different gifts, according to the grace given us. If a man's gift is prophesying, let him use it in proportion to his faith. If it is serving, let him serve; if it is teaching, let him teach; if it is encouraging, let him encourage; if it is contributing to the needs of others, let him give generously; if it is leadership, let him govern diligently; if it is showing mercy, let him do it cheerfully. (Romans 12:4-8)

This is only a partial list of the many gifts and talents you may possess for the Lord's service. Just as the body needs each of its different parts to function for the good of all, so the body of Christ requires each of us to do our part and do it with joy.

Time is an equally important area of our commitment. Time has become one of our culture's most valuable commodities. If our time goes only to fulfilling personal needs, we are not using this resource as God intended. There are many in our society who crave the time and attention of one who cares. Giving our time shows others that they are important and valued. It takes the focus from ourselves and leads us to recognize that even our time is a gift from the Lord. The giving of our time reminds us that we are asked to set aside our own needs and desires. We are to serve from our hearts.

The third area of giving involves our financial resources. How we use our money says a great deal about where our heart is. A disciplined race requires commitment to giving of our financial resources. Without a commitment in this area, it is easy to find that all of our money has disappeared before we have given anything to support God's work. Our money is a gift from the Lord, and responsible, joyful giving is an important part of a solid spiritual training plan.

As we train for our race, giving and serving reveal a depth of character and integrity within us. Are your deeds demonstrating your faith? Are you living with the lifeblood of a servant's heart?

sTRETCHING oUT

Describe some talents or abilities you believe God has given you to serve others in His name.

Brainstorm a list of ways you could give of your time.

How will you commit to give of your money to the Lord's
work?

Lighting Your World

Imagine you are in a huge stadium, and every
seat is filled. The sun has set, and the last glimmer of its
golden rays has just disappeared below the horizon. The
entire stadium sits in darkness, and a hush settles over
the crowd. A single runner enters the stadium carrying a
lighted torch. The runner is illuminated by the glow of the
torch, and a sense of anticipation trickles through the
stands. Although each person in the stadium has been
given a candle, the candles remain unlit, and the crowd
remains blanketed in thick darkness. You watch as the
runner slowly makes his way around the track. Your eyes
are glued to the one blazing light that breaks through a
new patch of darkness with each step he takes.

After circling the entire arena, the runner stops
and walks confidently toward an older woman seated in
the front row. He reaches out and lights her candle, then
steps back. The woman turns and lights the candle held
by the person next to her, and so on. The light spreads,
one candle at a time, until the entire stadium is bathed in
glowing candlelight. What started with one torch grew
quickly to illuminate an entire stadium.

As Christians, we are called to be light bearers in
our world and to share the light that God gave us. In
2 Corinthians 4:4–6, we read:

> The god of this age has blinded the minds of unbelievers, so that they cannot see the light of the gospel of the glory of Christ, who is the image of God. For we do not preach ourselves, but Jesus Christ as Lord, and ourselves as your servants for Jesus' sake. For God, who said, "Let light shine out of darkness," made His light shine in our hearts to give us the light of the knowledge of the glory of God in the face of Christ.

We live in a world that needs the Savior. We who follow Him have received His light, and with it, the privilege of passing it on. Like the runner in our story, sharing our light has a far-reaching impact. In the book of Matthew, Jesus proclaims:

> "You are the light of the world. A city on a hill cannot be hidden. Neither do people light a lamp and put it under a bowl. Instead they put it on its stand, and it gives light to everyone in the house. In the same way, let your light shine before men, that they may see your good deeds and praise your Father in heaven." (Matthew 5:14-16)

These verses state that one Light brought light to everyone in the house. These verses also remind us that a light is not to be hidden, but it is to shine forth so God might be praised and glorified.

God wants all people to know Him and to be saved. In Matthew 28:19, Jesus says, "Therefore go and make disciples of all nations." He calls us to work with Him to spread the light and to share His love and the life-giving message He offers.

As we run the race of faith, we spread Christ's light and love through how we live, what we do, and what we say. We communicate the Gospel message in many ways, and God opens doors in many places. You may

166

have an opportunity to talk with someone and share your Christian faith—what Jesus means to you. Perhaps you will reach out with compassion or forgive even when forgiveness is undeserved and people will see the light of Christ in your actions. Others may simply watch how you live from day-to-day and notice something different about you, something they want. They might see a deep sense of peace regardless of circumstances, a confident sense of purpose, or values that place the needs of others ahead of your own.

Imagine yourself carrying a torch wherever you go, bringing light to dark places. What Jesus has to offer can't be found in anyone or anything else, and each of us has the privilege of sharing with others the gift and blessings of our Savior, Jesus Christ. Are you ready to "spread the light"?

STRETCHING OUT

What are some "dark places" in which God might want to use you to spread His light?

This is what I would like others to know about Jesus ...

List ways you could tell others about Jesus and the message of the Gospel. Who will be the real power behind what you do?

RUNNING THE RACE:
THE ONGOING CHALLENGE

Today we're going to take a brief lap around the track. We'll be reviewing what we have talked about in this book and challenging ourselves to think through the information we have learned and the goals for which we will continue to strive.

✗ **In the grandstand** are people of faith whom you can look to for inspiration and encouragement. You are also in the grandstand at times to cheer and encourage others.

✗ **Keep the end in mind** with a clear statement of the God-given purpose for your life.

✗ **Check your baggage** at the foot of the cross and don't let unnecessary burdens weigh you down. Jesus took all your sins away!

✗ **Avoid the tangles** strewn along your path so you may not be tripped up in your journey of faith.

✗ **Stick with your faith** no matter what happens, drawing on the strength and perseverance that Jesus offers through the Holy Spirit.

✗ **Be aware of the signs along the way** that remind you of your important calling to live a life of love.

✗ As you journey, remember always to **fix your eyes on Jesus** so you will see Him clearly.

✗ Follow your **spiritual training plan,** revising as you continue to grow, guided always by the presence and power of the Holy Spirit.

In the Grandstand

> Therefore, since we are surrounded by such a great cloud of witnesses. (Hebrews 12:1)

Who are people of faith to whom you can look for inspiration and encouragement?

Who are you cheering on and encouraging in his or her race of faith? How are you doing this?

Keeping the End in Mind

Write out your final purpose statement

How has the Holy Spirit continued to help you fulfill your God-given purpose?

Check Your Baggage

> Let us throw off everything
> that hinders. (Hebrews 12:1)

What baggage has the Holy Spirit helped you to leave at Jesus' cross?

What baggage is continuing to weigh you down in your race of faith?

Avoiding the Tangles

> And the sin that so easily
> entangles ... (Hebrews 12:1)

What are some stumbling blocks that the Holy Spirit has helped you to avoid?

Who or what continues to trip you up and cause you to stumble?

Sticking with It

> And let us run with perseverance.
> (Hebrews 12:1)

In what part of your life has the Holy Spirit led you to persevere?

In what part of your life do you need perseverance right now?

Signs along the Way

> The race marked out for us ...
> (Hebrews 12:1)

How has the Holy Spirit led you to practice the kind of love described in 1 Corinthians 13?

What areas still need improvement?

Fixing Our Eyes on Jesus

> Let us fix our eyes on Jesus, the author and perfecter of our faith, who for the joy set before Him endured the cross, scorning its shame, and sat down at the right hand of the throne of God.
> (Hebrews 12:2)

What are some distractions that draw your eyes and your heart away from Jesus?

How has the Holy Spirit helped you to fix your eyes on Jesus?

PUTTING IT ALL TOGETHER

My Spiritual Training Plan

Purpose Statement for My Life:

My commitment to follow Jesus through the power of the Holy Spirit:

My commitment to quiet time with the Lord:

The time and place I will reserve for my quiet time with the Lord:

Resource(s) from which I will study:

My commitment to prayer as a part of my quiet time:

My commitment to worship and group participation:

My commitment to attend the Lord's Supper:

My commitment to giving and serving:

Time

Abilities and talents

Money

My Commitment to Spread the Light: